Frank Hudson

**She shall be mine!**

Vol. I

Frank Hudson

**She shall be mine!**
*Vol. I*

ISBN/EAN: 9783337052874

Printed in Europe, USA, Canada, Australia, Japan

Cover: Foto ©ninafisch / pixelio.de

More available books at **www.hansebooks.com**

# SHE SHALL BE MINE!

## A Novel

BY

## FRANK HUDSON

AUTHOR OF "THE LAST HURDLE," ETC.

*IN TWO VOLUMES*
VOL. I

London
WARD AND DOWNEY, Ld.
12 YORK STREET COVENT GARDEN
1894

[*All rights reserved*]

TO

# ROBERT BUCHANAN,

*POET.   NOVELIST.   DRAMATIST.*

# CONTENTS OF VOLUME I.

| CHAP. | | PAGE |
|---|---|---|
| I. | THE TOLKA MILL | 1 |
| II. | SOME ONE IS COMING | 16 |
| III. | THE NEW GUEST | 25 |
| IV. | MR. WATTS IS WAKEFUL | 33 |
| V. | A SURPRISE | 43 |
| VI. | VERY STRANGE NEWS | 51 |
| VII. | AN IRISH EDITOR | 62 |
| VIII. | A MOST MYSTERIOUS OUTRAGE | 79 |
| IX. | LIZ AND SHAUN | 93 |
| X. | THE CHRISTENING | 103 |
| XI. | THE RESULTS OF NIGHT SHOOTING | 116 |
| XII. | LANGTON ARRIVES | 128 |
| XIII. | LANGTON'S FATE | 138 |
| XIV. | MY FATE | 147 |
| XV. | CAPTAIN TEMPEST | 158 |

## CONTENTS.

| CHAP. | | PAGE |
|---|---|---|
| XVI. | AT THE RACES | 167 |
| XVII. | I SCORE AGAINST THE CAPTAIN | 182 |
| XVIII. | GRANGE FOYLE | 192 |
| XIX. | LANGTON IS LANDED | 204 |
| XX. | BY ETHEL'S SIDE | 213 |
| XXI. | CAPTAIN TEMPEST RETIRES | 229 |
| XXII. | LIZ LEAVES US | 238 |
| XXIII. | ONCE MORE BESIDE HER | 247 |

# SHE SHALL BE MINE.

## CHAPTER I.

### THE TOLKA MILL.

As I step from the train on to the platform of Ballyboyle station, I am gratified by the welcome, sweet, healthy odour of pine trees; right from the back of the platform do these pines climb up the "Station Hill," until they form a feathery cloud against the evening sky. Crossing the footbridge, I reach the other side of the station, and there, down at my feet, lies Ballyboyle.

Ballyboyle, let me whisper, is only a

village, but it is not the acme of diplomacy to call it so—within five miles of its site. Within that radius it is always referred to as the "Town." It is built on the elongated plan, and consists of one long, wide High Street, and several short and narrow low ones—the latter being in fact mere lanes. Its staple manufactures are semi-nude *gossoons*, and a species of long-bodied dog, celebrated for the marvellous dexterity which it exhibits in scratching any portion of its body with its hind-leg. The public buildings consist of a police-barrack—a modest, unassuming structure, of the pure, early Victorian period, with its whitewashed frontage, and its cabbage-garden; a red-brick post-office and general emporium— you can get anything in it, from a stamp to a ton of coals, from a trout-fly to the last edition of Tennyson, from a patent coffin to half-a-pound of tea. Duffey's public-house, which completes the "lions," is locally known as Mr. Duffey's Hotel. It is very small and very dark, and its bar is only big enough to hold Mrs. Duffey, a canary in a square cage, two or three dozen tumblers and pewter pints, and Duffey's cat, who sits purring at the canary, or catching flies in the window, on the rare occasions in which she is not engaged in having kittens. The little square space through which Mrs. Duffey dispenses refreshments is only wide enough for two of her customers to look through together, so the residue are forced to spread themselves into the tap-room and talk politics. Mrs. Duffey is square-figured, red-faced, and black-eyed. She "got her schoolin'" in Dublin, and consequently would not say "tay" for the world! Her husband is a grey-haired, dapper old chap, who devotes his time to buying and selling horses, leaving the entire management of the HOTEL to his wife.

But all this time I am bowling along per car to the Tolka Mill—distant some four miles from Ballyboyle—with my modest luggage, a portmanteau, trout-rod, and landing-net, for the Tolka is famous for its fat brown trout, and season after season have I spent in tempting them. The mill is tenanted by one Bartle McBride, whose wife believes strongly in the business of money-making, and has had a portion of the old rambling mill-house furnished for the accommodation of anglers.

The driver of my car is a little old chap, with a face like a dried apple. The major portion of his coat consists of holes, and his antique beaver hat has evidently descended from his grandfather.

"Well, Tim, how have things been going on since I was here last?" I presently ask.

"Oh, rightly, Mr. Dolan, rightly, sur— only Mrs. McBride herself isn't out iv her bed since Friday."

"Indeed!" I say. "So she is ill. I hope it is nothing serious, Tim?"

"No, Mr. Dolan, sur, it's nothin' sarious," Tim answers slowly—"nothin' sarious, be no manner iv manes."

"I am very glad to hear that, Tim. Is it a slight cold?"

"No, indeed thin, it is not, sur."

"No? An accident, perhaps?"

"No, sur, nor an accident nayther." And then, after a pause—"Shure, she had a young son a Thursday night."

"What!" I exclaim in astonishment.

"The divil a word iv a lie in it!" continues Tim with a grin. "An' afther tin year! Doesn't it bait all? But she was always a wonderful woman, sur— always a wonderful woman. The divil a know you'd iver know *what* she was up to!"

"I presume that Bartle was somewhat surprised, Tim?"

"Surprised, sur! He was fairly mismerized, that's what he was. Av coorse he had to stand thrate to all the boys, you may be shure!"

"I suppose Bartle has engaged a servant to look after myself and other anglers," I say.

"Sorra a know I know, sur," replies Tim. "I was jist thinkin' to meself how *you* war goin' to git on, wid herself not there to attind upon you."

"By Jove, Tim, that's a very serious question!"

"It is, sur—most sarious." And so saying Tim drives me up to the millhouse.

Bartle, highly floured from head to

foot, meets me at the door with a bashful grin.

"Av coorse you have heerd the news, Mr. Dolan," he says, lifting my portmanteau.

"Oh, indeed I have, Bartle—allow me to congratulate you. I hope both mother and son are progressing favourably?"

"Oh, yis, sur, thank you kindly; herself is goin' on fine. The babby is doin' rightly too; but Lord save me sowl, it cries a power! But they do cry, thim babbies, you know, sur. Some iv them, I'm towld, is divils at it."

And after giving me this item of information, Bartle disappears with my traps, while I enter the sitting-room. I can see that it has been newly dusted and "set to rights." Moreover, the few ornaments which it boasts on side-table and chimney-piece are more artistically arranged than ever they were before. Bartle is evidently a finished parlour-maid. Here he comes.

"What will you have for your dinner, sur, an' whin will you have it?" he wants to know.

"What can you give me?" I ask.

"Would you like some fried trouts, sur, wid a roast fowl to folla?"

"The very thing!" I declare, wondering the while where the cook is to come from.

"Very good, sur—it will be ready be siven."

"That's the style!"

"Yis, sur," acquiesces Bartle. "But won't you go up an' see if your bedroom is to your likin'?"

Thus appealed to, I proceed up-stairs to my room. If I was surprised at the taste displayed in the arrangement of the sitting-room, I am doubly so here. Bunches of sweet spring flowers on either side of the dressing-table; pens, ink, and paper on the side-table; every fold in blind and curtains arranged for artistic effect. Bartle *is* a wonderful man!

Presently I sally out for a stroll round the old place. The mill-building starts from behind the dwelling-house, and straggles along for about sixty yards. Its brown fat wheel is fed by a "race" from the high level of the Tolka, and the water, after doing its duty, escapes by a gully back again to its parent in the lower level. This lower level is the chosen play-ground and feeding-ground of the trout, ay, and of silver-sided salmon to boot, not to mention an odd pike or two lying perdu among the flags and lilies down there by the bridge.

By and by I return to the house. When I enter the sitting-room (and dining-room) it is to find my dinner-table arranged in a manner which would do credit to a Carlton Club waiter. A bright turf fire burns in the grate, for the evenings are still cold.

Presently I hear the welcome sound of the dinner-tray, followed by the entrance of *such* a waiting-maid! Tall, golden-haired, blue-eyed, and with a complexion like a fresh peach. Young she is too—not more than seventeen. She is dressed in black, relieved by a little white apron. Deftly she takes the dish of trout from the tray, places it on the table, arranges my plate, draws a chair, and then turning to me, says—

"Would you kindly ring when you require the fowl, sir?"

"Yes," I answer, and she retires.

Her accent, I noticed, was refined and decidedly English. Probably she has been in service in some Belgravian mansion. But then, how came she to this out-of-the-way place? I have it! She is a professional nurse sent by the doctor to attend upon Mrs. McBride. No, on second thoughts that idea is not feasible. Anyhow, wherever she came from, she knows how to cook trout.

In due time I ring for the fowl, and the fair unknown enters with it. When she has placed it before me, and is leaving with the tray, she turns and says—

"I hope you liked the trout, sir."

"Yes, my dear, very much," I declare. "Never tasted better in my life."

"I am glad to hear you say so, sir," and away she goes.

And by and by, when she comes to clear the table, I notice that she keeps her eyes downcast, nor does she seem to be aware of my presence, as I sit by the fire pipe in mouth. But when she is leaving with the crowded tray I rise and open the door for her, and make her smile at last.

"Thank you, sir," she says, displaying a white flash of teeth. "Will you require coffee?"

"No, but I shall want some hot water for punch—say in fifteen minutes."

As she retires I go up-stairs to my room for the whisky, and presently return with a flask filled with real " J. J." from Mooney's —warranted ten years old.

When the fair unknown brings the hot water and tumbler—not forgetting the sugar and lemon—I proceed to mix a glass of punch.

"Now, I don't think I'll have to trouble you any more to-night," I say.

"Very well, sir," she answers, and ere she goes takes up the snuffers and attempts to snuff the old-fashioned candles. The first one she manages to snuff all right, but the other one she extinguishes altogether.

"Ah, you are not accustomed to old-fashioned candles," I observe. "*West End* candles require no snuffers."

"Do you mean the West End of London, sir?" she asks, relighting the candle.

"Yes."

"I have never been there, sir," and she cautiously proceeds to snuff the other candle.

"No! well, really, I was under the impression that you had just come from there."

"Why, sir?" she wants to know, while the faint glimmer of a smile flits round her lips.

"Why? Well, your appearance—your—your general bearing gave me the impression."

She busies herself for a moment, setting

the fire-irons in their proper places, and then with a " Good-night, sir," leaves me.

Curious sort of girl—very.

There are no newspapers to be had here, in fact, such things are quite unknown, which accounts for the heavenly peace and salubrity of the place. At the same time, I wish I had something to read just now. I read through the family library here during my last visit, when it rained without ceasing for three weeks. Said library consists of eight works in various states of preservation. They are as follows—*Collier the Robber, Irish Songs and Ballads, The Battle of Aughrim, Complete Farrier, Trojan Wars and Troy's Destruction, Life and Adventures of James Ferney, Bonaparte's Oraculam, Hocus Pocus, or the Whole Art of Legerdemain.*

I think I will have another dip into *James Ferney;* it is one of——

Knock at the door, followed by the entrance of the fair unknown, to ask me concerning breakfast-hour.

"Nine o'clock, my dear."

She does not like being called "my dear," I can divine. Very well, I shall not call her so again.

## CHAPTER II.

### SOME ONE IS COMING.

WHILE at breakfast this morning I asked the fair unknown what her name was.

"Alice," she answered quickly.

"Well, Alice, how is Mrs. McBride this morning?"

"She is progressing most favourably, the doctor asserts, sir."

"And the baby?"

"Oh, he is *quite* well," she declared, with a smile. "I hope he did not disturb you, sir? His lungs are particularly strong."

"No," I answered, laughing, "he did not disturb me in the least. He has a nurse, I presume?"

"Oh, yes, sir; Mrs. McBride's nurse also waits on *him*." And so saying Alice left me to myself.

  \*  \*  \*  \*  \*

I have had a good time of it with the trout, and am on my way back to the mill, when I meet Bartle McBride.

"Morrah, Mr. Dolan!" he exclaims. "Begorra, I see you have cotch a few good wans th' day."

"Yes, Bartle, I have had fair sport."

"I hope you are comfortable, an' plaised wid your room an' all," he continues.

"Indeed I am, Bartle," I say. "By the way, that is a capital servant-maid you have got. Her cooking and attendance are perfect."

"I'm right glad to hear you say that, sur," answers the miller.

"Where did she come from?" I ask.

"Why—from Dublin, iv coorse," he

answers, after a pause—"from Dublin, iv coorse, sur. Yarragh, but thim is mortyal fine trouts you have! They are so, an' no mistake!" And Bartle appears greatly interested in the contents of my creel. "But shure your lunch must be waitin' for you, Mr. Dolan, so hurry in," and away he trudges without waiting to hear another word.

After luncheon I am strolling about the mill, pipe in mouth, when I come upon Mick O'Brien. Mick is Bartle's right-hand man, and is quite as much disguised in flour as his master is. During my last visit here Mick regaled me with numerous anecdotes concerning his son Patsey, who, according to all accounts, is a regular genius.

"Well, Mick, how is your son getting on at school?"

"Oh, begorra, sur, he's goin' on fine!"

Mick affirms proudly. "Yarragh, but it's himself that 'ill be the knowledgable man whin he grows big!"

"And what age is he now, Mick?"

"Thirteen come next St. Patrick's day, sur. An', me dear, but it's himself that has the book-larnin'."

"Do you tell me so, Mick?"

"Faith, I do, Mr. Dolan, sur! An' shure wait till I tell you. Dother day the master towld all the scolards in the school to write down on paper all they knew consarnin' cats."

"Write down? Oh, I understand—they were to write an essay on cats."

"Yis, sur, I bleeve that's what they call it. Well, wait till I show you what our Patsey writ; begorra, you'll die wid surprise! Shure it's good enough for prent, that's what it is."

And Mick fumbles in his pocket, and at

length produces a large sheet of foolscap, which he unfolds and hands to me, saying with pride beaming from his old grey eyes—

"There you are, Mr. Dolan, sur—jist read that, an' it 'll show you what our Patsey can do."

The essay is written in a big fat hand. I leave the orthography as it stands in all its native originality. The syntactic beauty of the construction of several sentences I also shrink from tampering with. All I conventionalize is the punctuation.

### "Cats.

"Cats has 4 claws, an wan hed an tale, also a body cuverd wid hair. Cats is iv too kinds—yalla, an black-an-white. They also has whiskers. Cats aits ivery thing they can lay there hands on, sich as rats an mise, an all thim Soort iv Things, also flis an bakon an mate. Most extronry thing, cats likes fishis, tho they hates wather. So, iv coorse, you may be shure they dont git much fishis to ait, excep thim which is coch an put on a dish in your mudder's pantry. Som Cats is all ways havin kitins, excep Tom Cats, which niver has eny. Tom Cats is the divils for fitin, and ken See better be nite nor day. Cats wont tuch you if you ony lave thim alone, an dont stand on there Tales. But, iv coorse, if you stand on there Tales they will turn round an scrob you, and the divil skewr to you! Cats has 9 lifes, but ony wan at a time. If Cats had more thin wan life at a time they wood not kno what to do wid thim all. Wan life at a time is enuf for eny baste, same as men and wimin. Bad boys thros stones at Cats, for which they will go to hel an burn for iver an iver, Amen! There was wanst in the sweet town iv Kilkiny 2 Cats, an 2 bad boys tide there tales together an slung thim acros a line for divarshion, an they ett aich other up, an left nothin ony there Tales, for which thim 2 bad boys aut to have got 6 monts, but they didn't. We wanst had a cat in our house, an it bet all! It wood sleep no where ony on me mudder's chest. Me mudder didn't mind it a bit, becaze she was ust to it, but me fathr woodn't stand it at all, an ust to ketch it be the tale an sling it ut iv the bed 20 times a nite. That's all I kno about Cats. Patsey O'Brien."

"Very good, very good indeed, Mick," I say, handing him back the paper. "Your son bids fair to become a great humourist."

"An' what soort iv a thing is that, sur?" asks Mick, carefully folding the paper and replacing it in his pocket.

"Oh, a humourist is one who takes an original view of anything."

"Ay, sur," says Mick, " that's jist what our Patsey does. Shure, didn't he up an' tell me dother day that the moon wasn't a moon at all, at all! 'Clare to faith he did, sur! Said the moon was a worrld jist like this, on'y all life was distinct upon it."

" Distinct ? "

" Yis, sur, that's what he towld me."

" He was probably quite right, Mick."

" Is that so, sur ? " and Mick looks at me gravely. " Begorra, I scarce could believe him, on'y I didn't like to tell him so."

Leaving Mick to ponder over his son's astronomical knowledge, I wander into the garden, and presently come upon Alice, who is gathering a bunch of flowers. Prettier than ever does she look in a natty little hat trimmed with pink ribbons.

" You remind me of the goddess Flora," I say, stopping in my walk.

"I am endeavouring to collect enough blossoms for our new guest's room, sir," she answers.

"New guest?"

"Yes, sir; Mr. McBride has just received a letter from Dublin. Some gentleman is coming down for a couple of weeks, and will arrive to-night."

"I'm glad to hear that," I say.

"I suppose you are, sir; I dare say you begin to feel lonely."

"No, I don't feel exactly lonely, but still, I am glad to hear that some fellow is coming. By the way, Alice, how do *you* like being here?"

"Oh, I like the place very well, sir," she murmurs, after a moment spent in arranging some of the flowers in the bunch.

The next moment she is walking down the path towards the gate.

## CHAPTER III.

### THE NEW GUEST.

The old clock in the hall is striking ten o'clock when the new guest arrives, accompanied by a trout-rod, landing-net, and travelling-bag.

He is a jovial-looking, smooth-faced man, and speaks with a strong North Dublin brogue. But for his unclerical suit of Blarney tweed, I would take him to be a priest. I notice that he is slightly lame, and uses a stick as he walks towards the fire.

"Good-night, sir," he says, beaming upon me with good humour. "Isn't it lovely weather we're havin'?" And he sinks into the chair with a happy smile.

He has evidently received a fortnight's vacation from his employers, and feels all the pleasure of a school-boy just home for the holidays.

"Yes, we are having splendid weather just now," I say, "though the nights are still cold."

"Ah, what matter for that?" he asks. "What matter for that, me dear sur? Better have the cold nights now, and have done with them before the real summer comes. How is the river?—that's the main question."

"The river is in splendid form," I tell him. "I landed six beauties to-day."

His eyes sparkle on hearing this—he is evidently an enthusiast.

"I love fishing!" he declares. "Love it! Even when I was a boy, I many a time mitched from school to ketch eels in the Grand Canal in Dublin." And he laughs at the remembrance. "Many's the thrashin' I got for my pains."

"Have you ever been down here before?" I ask.

"Oh, yes, about five years ago—before I went to me present employment. I don't get a chance of much fishing now, but last month I fell and hurt me leg, and was confined to bed for three weeks. Then I thought I'd go back to work again, but soon discovered that I wasn't quite cured, so they gave me a fortnight's holiday, and here I am."

"Well, I hope you will return all sound and well," I say.

"Oh, I'm full sure of that," he replies—"full sure. But I wish they would bring me the tea." And he looks wistfully towards the door. "It's rather late for tea, sur, but somehow it's the only thing I feel a wish for after my journey."

"Will you not find it rather sleep-dispelling?" I ask.

"Ah, not at all, sur," he answers, smiling. "Nothing keeps me from me natural rest, thank God! I will be up and after the trout long before breakfast."

Presently Alice enters with the tea; as she arranges the tray the stranger casually turns to look at her. Perhaps it is imagination on my part, but I could almost swear that he gives a slight start on seeing her. However, he turns towards the fire again, saying to me—

"What sort of a fly did they take to-day, sur?"

I tell him; and then Alice, drawing a chair to the table, says—

"Your tea is now ready, sir."

"Thanks," he answers, rising and taking his place at the table.

"Will you know your room, sir?" she asks.

"Oh, indeed I will," he answers, as he pours out the tea. "The first on the right of the landing—Mr. McBride told me. Sure, I had the same room when I was here before."

"You will find the candle and matches on the hall table, sir," Alice tells him.

"Thanks," says the stranger, now busy with the loaf. "Good-night."

"Rather a nice-looking girl," I venture to remark, when Alice has gone.

"Yes, indeed," he replies. "Seems a high cut above a mill servant,—don't you think so?"

"Yes; have you noticed how refined her accent is?"

"I have, sur; and I have also noticed that she is an English girl."

"Oh, yes, there is no mistaking her nationality."

"I suppose you don't know how she comes to be here?" he asks.

"Not in the least."

"No, I suppose not," he continues. "That, of course, is her own business."

And so saying he devotes his entire attention to his tea.

When he has finished he returns to the chair by the fire, and lights his pipe.

"Ah," he exclaims, "I feel much better now."

"Yes, tea is a famous reviver," I say.

"It is that, sur—it is that."

He smokes with a look of joyous content for a few minutes, and then asks—

"I suppose you never see a newspaper here?"

"No, thank goodness," I answer. "I don't believe I would open one if I saw it lying before me."

He laughs at this, and then plunges

into politics. I find him to be an out-and-out Nationalist. How he inveighs against the poor English Government! Not being a politician, I gently play him back to the gentle art. He is a willing captive, and is soon deep in piscatorial data.

"Do you ever fish for salmon?" he suddenly asks.

"Sometimes."

"Well, look here, me dear sur, I'll just give you a wrinkle. If ever you want to ketch salmon in an Irish river, no matter the divil where it runs, use a live collien-fasough."

"A live what?" I exclaim.

"A live collien-fasough, sur. It is an Irish word, and means 'old woman in the ditch.' It is a little fish like a small gudgeon, and is found in most ditches and streams in Ireland. It's a dead bait for salmon and pike. A trout in the flood-time will take it too—but it must be a big one that does."

"Ah, I must try it," I say.

"Take my advice, and do, sur," he continues. "Take my advice, and do."

Here he looks at his watch, and stating that it is time for all good people to be in bed, rises and wishes me good-night. It is not long ere I follow his example, and get between the sheets.

## CHAPTER IV.

### MR. WATTS IS WAKEFUL.

THE morning sun shines warm and bright, and the hall clock is striking the hour of nine in its old-fashioned, slow, solemn, vibrating way, as I enter the sitting-room. Presently Alice appears with the tray.

" Good-morning, Alice—you are looking even more lovely than ever this morning."

She does not hear me, of course, and I add—

" Where is our new lodger? Oh, I forgot —he said he would go a-fishing before breakfast. Some one ought to go down to the river and remind him of breakfast, for he is such an enthusiast he will forget all about the matter. By the way, Alice, what is the gentleman's name?"

"Mr. Watts," Alice answers; "but he is not fishing this morning, sir."

"No!" I say in surprise. "Then what the deuce is he doing—still slumbering?"

"No, sir; he drove into Ballyboyle early this morning."

"Drove into Ballyboyle! Why, what on earth did he do that for?"

"I believe he lost a portion of his luggage," she answers, pouring out my tea— "a hat-box or something of the sort, and thought it best to report the matter at once. He said he would be back by breakfast-time."

And sure enough, at this moment the sound of wheels is heard, and in another minute or so Mr. Watts limps into the sitting-room, beaming with good-humour.

"Back in time, you see!" he exclaims to Alice. "And as hungry as a pike."

Alice leaves to prepare his breakfast, and I say—

"I thought you told me you were going to have a whip at the river before breakfast this morning?"

"Ah, shure, so I was—so I was, sur," he answers, as he draws a chair to the table. "But when I went to me room last night, I discovered that one of me traps were missing, so I thought it best to drive over to the station at once, and report the matter."

"Well, had they got it there?"

"No, but they will make inquiries about it. And now, tell me, what part of the river are you going to take?"

"Beyond the bridge," I answer.

"Very well; I'll take the near side. There is no use in us both sticking too close together—no use at all; though it would be more pleasant, of course."

"You are quite right," I say.

Here Alice brings in his breakfast, and presently, mine being finished, I start alone for the river.

\* \* \* \* \*

We do not meet again until dinner-time, when, on comparing our creels, I discover that Mr. Watts has beaten me by three. How he *does* enjoy it!

"Ah, I'm the boy for them, lame and all as I am!" he cries. "They know *me!*"

During dinner he dilates on the various dodges for luring trout, and gives me some really valuable hints. From fish he wanders to birds and bird-trapping.

"Ireland has always been the divil's own place for birds," he declares. "And every boy in the country is an expert trapper."

"Oh, indeed, I know that," I say. "When I was a boy it was my favourite hobby."

"Ah, it's rare fun!" he continues. "Did you ever eat a sparrow pie?"

"No, I don't think I ever did."

"Faith, then, I can tell you what it is, sur, it's *gallopshish*—that's what it is! But what me and the other young chaps used to do, was roll them in mud, and then throw them into the centre of a bright turf fire. When we saw the mud cracking we knew the sparrow was cooked to a turn, and used to take them out one by one with a tongs. Then when we took the caked mud off, there was the sparrow, white as snow and soft as butter."

"I suppose you used to have regular banquets?" I say.

"Rather!" and Mr. Watts's eyes sparkle at the remembrance of boyhood's happy days.

And so we continue on topics of birds, beasts, and fishes until dinner is over. Then we draw chairs to the fire, and light our pipes.

Coming on towards ten o'clock Mr. Watts became rather silent, and once or twice I fancy he seems to be *listening* for some sound. Presently he casually asks—

"I suppose the last post from Dublin would have time to reach here by this?"

"The last post from Dublin reach *here!*" I exclaim in astonishment.

"No, no, I don't mean that," he says quickly—"I don't mean that. Of course no letter would be forwarded here tonight."

"Certainly not—unless you left instructions at the post-office to have it forwarded by special car, which would be rather an expensive way of receiving a letter."

"You are right, sur," says Mr. Watts. "And even if a man did do that, he wouldn't get the letter much before now."

While he speaks, the noise of wheels disturbs the dogs and geese in the mill-yard, and in a few moments Alice enters the room bearing a long official-looking envelope.

"For you, sir," she says, handing it to Mr. Watts. "The carman says that there is five shillings to pay."

"Oh, yes," answers Mr. Watts, producing the money and handing it to her. "There you are."

She takes the money and leaves.

"So you *were* expecting a letter," I say.

"Well, yes," he answers, "I was, but I was not sure of its coming to-night."

"Rather expensive—five shillings, eh?"

"It is indeed," he replies—"it is indeed, but it is rather important. Now I'm off to bed; good-night, sur."

And away he goes, without having opened that important letter.

I have another pipe, and then, feeling lonely, rise and go towards my room. As I reach the landing I catch sight of Mr. Watts walking quickly towards his room. Alice is standing at her room door. She turns towards me for a moment ere she retires and shuts the door; her face is as white as snow.

When I enter my room that white face seems to haunt me. Can it be that the work here is too heavy for her? No, I don't think so; neither Mr. Watts nor myself require very much attention.

There, I have left my keys on the table in the sitting-room! No help for it but to go down and get them.

Down-stairs I steal in my slippers, candle in hand. Just as I reach the bottom step some one rushes forth from the sitting-room and confronts me. It is Mr. Watts!

" Oh, it's you, sur !" he exclaims.

"Yes, it is I," I say in surprise, as I follow him into the room.

"I thought it was some burglar," he continues.

"Burglar!" I echo. "Why, who ever heard of a burglar in an Irish mill-house? But what the deuce has brought you down here?"

"I might as well ask what brought you," he answers, smiling, as he sits down on a chair beside the door.

"Ah, you have me there, I confess; I have come to find my keys—see, here they are!"

"Well, my reason for coming down is because I don't feel sleepy," he says.

"Why, I thought you told me you always slept well."

"Oh, yes, so I do as a rule," he answers, preparing to light his pipe. "So I do as a rule, sur, but to-night I somehow or another feel wakeful. It must be the corned-beef— I knew I was eating too much of it, but I'm so fond of it."

"Ah, that may account for it," I say. "But why don't you sit over here, and rouse up the fire?"

"Oh, the room is so close—the room is so close, sur; that's why I'm sitting here."

"Well, I'm off," I say; "good-night."

"Good-night, sur—good-night!" answers Mr. Watts. "Pleasant dreams to you." And so I leave him.

## CHAPTER V.

### A SURPRISE.

When I enter the sitting-room this morning, I immediately notice that the breakfast-table is arranged in a very rough-and-ready fashion. Is Alice getting careless? I ring the bell, and presently the breakfast tray arrives, carried by Bartle McBride!

"What, *you*, Bartle!" I exclaim in surprise. "Why, where is Alice?"

"She's gone, sur," he answers, laying down the tray, and gazing at me in a hopeless, bewildered way.

"Gone?"

"Yes, sur—her and Mr. Watts."

"And Mr. Watts?" I echo in astonishment. "How and when did they go?"

And the remembrance of the girl's white face and Watts's watchfulness comes back upon me. "Explain, Bartle."

"The divil a word I can explain at all, at all, Mr. Dolan, only this: at six this mornin' I was goin' on me way to the mill, an' was just passin' Alice's room, whin she opens the door, an' her fully dressed, wid hat an' all on. Av coorse I was surprised to see her, you may be sure, sur."

"Yes, go on."

"Well, sur, she sez, 'Mr. McBride, I'm sorry to have to lave you so suddin; would you mind takin' me trunk down to the hall?' I stood lookin' at her for a minit, an' sez, 'Arrah, what's the mainin' iv this, Alice?' An' she sez, 'Oh, plaze don't ask me any questions, Mr. McBride; I *must* go.' So wid that, sur, I ups an' carries her box down-stairs to the hall."

"And where was Mr. Watts?" I ask.

"Standin' waitin' in the hall, wid all his traps; an' whin he sees me he sez, 'Mr. McBride, I want your car at wanst, as me an' Alice has to ketch the half-a-past siven thrain for Dublin.' Well, Mr. Dolan, you could have knocked me down wid a feather, as I wint an' roused up Mick, an' he yoked the mare in a brace iv minits, an' druve the car round to the door. Thin Alice goes an' bids good-bye to Mrs. McBride, an' kisses the babby. Thin she comes an' shakes hands wid me. 'Good-bye, Mr. McBride,' she sez; 'an' remimber me to Mr. Dolan.' Thin Mr. Watts helped her on to the car, got up himself, an' I put her trunk up behind her, an' thin away they drove."

"Why, what does it all mean?" I ask.

"The divil a know *I* know, sur," answers Bartle, scratching the back of his floury head. "It's most mystarious, that's what it is. As purty a girl as iver the sun shone on. An' do you know what Mrs. McBride was sayin', sur?"

"What?"

"Why, she sez that Alice was only lettin' on, an' was no sarvint at all, but wan iv the quality. You know, Mr. Dolan, women can see through aich other like anything."

"I have an idea that Mrs. McBride is quite right," I say. "Did Mr. Watts pay his bill?"

"Oh, yis, sur, he did, an' said he might be back agin. But shure, ait your breakfast, Mr. Dolan, before it gets cold. Molly the nurse cooked it, so I don't think it will be too bad. But it took Alice to do things right. Yarrah, but she was the darlint."

Here Bartle retires and leaves me to myself. What can all this mean? Who was that man Watts, and what power had he over Alice? Who was she? Could it be a love affair between them? Why, the man was old enough to be her father.

With these thoughts chasing each other through my brain, I finish breakfast, and then go for a stroll. I am not in humour for angling to-day, so the trout in the Tolka can disport themselves in peace and safety. How I *hate* the mysterious! I would give a good round sum to know the solution of the Alice and Watts episode. Talk of Lytton's *Alice, or the Mysteries,* indeed! Here we have *Alice and Watts, or the Mystery.* Why, there are the germs of a whole novel in the very title.

In an hour's time I wander back to the house again, and sinking into a chair by the window, sit gazing on the geese as they persist, out of sheer eccentricity, in standing on one leg. If they had any mystery to bother their heads it might make them a trifle less eccentric. Ah, down goes the second leg all round! The noise of wheels is heard—louder, *louder*, LOUDER, until the geese scatter in all directions as a car drives up to the door. It is driven by old Tim, and carries, besides his venerable self, two strangers, who both jump down almost before the car stops. I rise, go to the hall door, and open it.

"Beg pardon," one of the strangers says in an unmistakable London accent, "is the miller at home?"

At this moment Bartle appears on the scene.

"Are you the miller?" asks the stranger, turning to him.

"I am, sur," answers Bartle.

"You have a lady stopping here—*this* lady," and he shows Bartle a photograph.

"Why, that's Alice!" exclaims Bartle.

"Yes," both the strangers exclaim together.

"Why, she's gone," continues the miller.

"Gone!" cry both strangers.

"Yis, wint off in a hurry this mornin'.

be the half-a-past siven thrain. Wint wid a jintleman by the name iv Mr. Watts."

"Done!" cries stranger number one to his companion. "Thank you—sorry for troubling you," he continues to Bartle.

"Don't mintion it, sur," answers the latter, and both the strangers quickly remount the car.

"Back to the station as quick as you can," one of them exclaims to Tim, who immediately starts at full speed, leaving Bartle and myself staring at each other in silent astonishment.

"Come in here," I say to him, after a pause, and he follows me into the sitting-room. "Now, Bartle, tell me truly, how did Alice come here to the mill-house?"

"Well, sir," begins Bartle, "she med Mrs. McBride and me promise to say nothin' to eny one at all consarnin' her; but shure, it's all wan now, so it is. She cum here as a lodger furst."

"A lodger?"

"Yis, sur. Av coorse, as you know, we advertise our fishin' accommodation ivery beginnin' iv the sayson in the *Field*, an' likewise the *Irish Times*. Well, sur, she seen our advertisement, an' so she cum here. But afther a while, sur, her money run short, poor thing, an' jist at the same time Mrs. McBride presinted me wid the babby. An' so Alice says, 'Mrs. McBride, I have no more money for a while, but if you like I'll stop here an' attind to the house affairs till sich times as you are able to do so yourself.' Av coorse, sur, Mrs. McBride was very glad iv the offer, an' now you know the whole story. But who the divil war them two that cum on the car? That bates all! I must go an' tell herself at wanst. I niver seen such goin's on before."

And away he goes to tell his wife all about the mysterious strangers.

## CHAPTER VI.

### VERY STRANGE NEWS.

Three weeks have gone by, and the summer has come. Mrs. McBride is once more visible, and bustles about the house with an energy which, I presume, is calculated to make up for any amount of lost time. She "looks after Mr. Dolan" with the greatest care and attention, though I wish the good lady would cease from continually questioning me on the Alice mystery.

"Lord save me sowl, Mr. Dolan, what's got the poor crayture?" is a query she puts to me at least ten times a day.

"I really don't know, Mrs. McBride," is my invariable answer.

"Well, I *do* wish some wan knew. The poor crayture!"

"Yes, it's very curious," I say, and then get out of her way.

I have been luring the trout ever since lunch time, and now the sun is thinking of setting, which suggests a rest and a pipe. Down I lie my length under a spreading beech by the running river. There is music in the air—the kind of music that Shakespeare loved. The drowsy hum of the mill, the melancholy mooing of distant kine, the chatter of the rooks up there on the tall elms which cap the hill, "the murmurings of innumerable bees," and the tristful coo of the wood-pigeon. There goes a kingfisher, like a flash of blue lightning up the water. A vole down by the flags on the opposite bank sits combing his whiskers. A thrush, after stopping his song to have a good look at me from the topmost branch of yonder chestnut, and assuring himself that I am not watching him, begins his glorious melody again. A big, fat, black-and-yellow bee comes buzzing across my face, almost hitting my pipe; the tobacco-smoke drives him away, but he returns again, and after making a tour round my feet, settles on a cowslip. Three white butterflies, on pleasure bent, flutter erratically round the tree trunk; and out there, hovering over a raft of water-lilies, his wings glistening like minute jewels, is a mighty dragon-fly, the merciless foe of all the hapless children of the sun who chance to come within his view. And——

A man comes slowly along, pipe in mouth and rod over shoulder—a merry-faced, curly-headed young fellow, with twinkling eyes and humorous mouth. His advent disturbs Mr. Vole from his toilet, that little gentleman disappearing like magic. Of course the thrush stops his song, and with head cocked on one side eyes the new-comer. The latter pauses, and looking up at the bird, exclaims—"Now then, Speckles, don't stop your lilt on my account! Is there a hole in the ballad?" Then turning to me he continues—"The little chap is terribly shy—the divil a sing he'll sing if he sees any one watching him."

"They all have that trait," I say. "If you sit down here quietly, and appear not to notice him, he will soon begin again."

"Ah, sure I know that," answers the stranger, sitting down beside me. "What a lovely evening it is! Did you ketch much?"

"A few," and I show him the contents of my creel.

"Ah, not too bad at all," he remarks.

"Better than me—I only landed three. What fly are you using?"

I show him my link, which he examines with much interest.

"Those are London made, sur," he says.

"Yes, I got them at Gold's, in Fleet Street."

"A good place, I'm told—a very good place, though I never saw it. Would you believe it, sur, when I tell you that I have never been out of Ireland in my life, except once, when I went as far as New York with the captain of a schooner I knew?"

"And you have never been in London?"

"Never in my life, sur,—and you'll think it strange that such is the case, when I tell you that I am a real live editor. They say that London is the Mecca of all Irish journalists."

"Yes," I say, "there are a vast number of Irishmen on the English press, and indeed they swarm in all the professions there—more especially in literature, music, and the drama. Are you a local editor, if I may ask the question?"

"Oh, indeed then, I am!" he answers, laughing; "I am Tom O'Hara, editor and proprietor of the *Ballyboyle Examiner*, at your service. I suppose you have come from London straight?"

"Yes, to enjoy some fishing—I am staying at the mill."

He is silent for a moment, and then he inquires—

"And have you been stopping long at the mill?"

"For about a month."

He is silent for another space; suddenly he says—

"Then I suppose you know all about that girl?"

"Do you mean Alice?" I ask.

"I don't know what her name was," he answers, "but she was a lovely creature! I never saw such eyes and hair." And then pausing for a minute, he adds, "I wonder what it was she did."

"Did?"

"Yes—what crime could such a young and beautiful creature have committed?"

"Crime!" I gasp.

"Yes," continued Mr. O'Hara, his look changing to one of surprise. "Why, didn't you know that she was arrested?"

"Arrested!" I cry, looking at him in amazement. "For heaven's sake tell me where you heard that!"

"Oh, faith, I can do that without much trouble," he answers. "I happened to be waiting for the first train to Dublin at the Ballyboyle station, and noticed a very lovely young lady with a lame gentleman. I was wondering who they could be, when Sargeant Boyle, who was on duty at the time, came up to me and whispered, 'I wonder what that girl has been up to?' I asked him what he meant, and he answered—'Don't you see she is under arrest—that man with her is a celebrated Dublin detective.' I was surprised, you may be sure."

"Good heavens!" I cry.

"They both travelled to Dublin first-class," Mr. O'Hara continues. "I went by the same train, but travelled second-class."

"Did you see them again when you arrived in Dublin?"

"Just for a moment; they entered a cab, but I don't know where it drove to."

I sit silent, and completely astounded. Alice a criminal! Watts a detective! The thought makes me actually shudder. Mr. O'Hara breaks the silence.

"By the way, sur, as I understand

from what you tell me, Bartle knows nothing about the girl's arrest."

"Nothing whatever," I say; "he is as ignorant on the matter as I was ere you enlightened me."

"Well then, don't say anything to him upon the matter—it would only worry him and his wife. That was my reason for not having anything about it in the *Examiner*—though it would have sold a few extra copies. But I withstood the temptation, because Bartle is a good sort of chap, and gives me liberty to fish here whenever I like."

"Never fear—they will hear nothing from me," I assure him. "But the whole affair is very sad."

"So it is—so it is, indeed," he answers. "I wonder what she *could* have been up to?"

"Heaven knows!"

"I wonder now, could she have been what they call an adventuress, or a member of the Swell Mob?"

"Oh, no—I do not believe such a thing for a moment."

"No, sur, I don't suppose you do—neither do I," continues Mr. O'Hara. "But it is a curious fact in nature, that you can never tell whether those very fair women are good or bad. A man can tell well enough, by the expression of a brunette's eyes, what sort of a woman she is, but a fair-haired, blue-eyed beauty may be either an angel or a devil, and you won't know it until you are married to her—the divil a know."

Here that thrush ventures to begin his song once again, and somehow his singing makes me feel anything but cheerful, so I rise to return to the house.

"Are you off?" asks Mr. O'Hara.

"Yes, I have had enough of fishing for to-day."

"Well, Mr.———"

"Dolan."

"Well, Mr. Dolan, if you feel that way inclined, you might drop over to Ballyboyle some day and have a bit of dinner at my humble abode. You can meet me at my office in the High Street—anybody will show it to you. Will you come?—you might as well."

"Well, then, you come and have dinner with me now," I answer, glad of having some one to keep me in countenance.

"Right you are!" he exclaims, jumping up and shouldering his rod.

And in another moment we are crossing the meadow towards the mill-house, Mr. O'Hara the while humming,

"Do not forget me, do not forget me,
Do not forget me, the Maid of the Mill."

## CHAPTER VII.

### AN IRISH EDITOR.

Mrs. McBride meets us at the door.

"Ah, thin, an' how are you th' day, Mr. O'Hara?" she asks.

"Oh, faith, I'm in prime condition, Mrs. McBride," he replied—"fit as a three-year-old. I suppose Bartle is as proud as a ten-shilling teapot at the son-and-heir? How goes the little chap?"

"Begorra, he's finely, sur,—but shure, why didn't you drop in on your way to the river?"

"Faith, I don't know why I didn't," is Mr. O'Hara's very truthful reply.

"Now, Mrs. McBride," I say; "Mr. O'Hara is going to dine with me, and we are both as hungry as hawks, so let us have dinner as soon as you like."

"That I will, sur," and away she bustles.

"She is one of the best wives in the county," declares the editor—"one of the very best. I put the birth of the son at the top of a column, and had a five-line par in the Local Gossip into the bargain."

"That was very good," I say, and then go in search of the whisky-bottle. Returning with it I give it into Mr. O'Hara's care, while I go and fish for two tumblers and the water-bottle. These items being secured, we sit on the rustic seat outside the windows, and enjoy a pipe and a glass—an Irish pre-prandial digestive.

"I don't suppose you have many exciting events to chronicle in your paper as a rule?" I say.

"No, indeed," answers the editor, in a

tone of deep regretfulness. "The country about here is far too quiet—that's what it is! Not like the good old times! Why, Mr. Dolan, about ten years ago there was a fierce agrarian war in full swing in this county, and it nearly made my fortune."

"Indeed!"

"Yes, sur, that's a fact; there were at least two or three agents peppered with great regularity every week, and sometimes an odd landlord was popped at, besides kishloads of threatening letters. I tell you, our machines were kept busy, and no mistake. In fact, everything in our town was kept busy; for what with the extra police, and, above all, the dragoons, why, business was brisk all round. But now everything and everybody in Ballyboyle appears to be asleep."

"The dragoons?" I query. "I was not aware of any barracks in Ballyboyle."

"No, there is no real military barracks, but they fitted up the old market-house for the men, and the horses were stabled in Duffy's. Ah, those were the times!" and Mr. O'Hara heaves a sigh.

"I suppose you do not go in for the new journalism?" I casually ask.

"What's that?"

"Why, the Interview System."

"Ah, no," says Mr. O'Hara; "it wouldn't answer. You see, Mr. Dolan, there is nobody about these parts who knows anything worth interviewing him about. Every man in the place knows his neighbour's business; and as for the women — why, they know more about each other than they do themselves."

I do not quite follow the intricate meaning of the last sentence, but refrain from mentioning the fact to Mr. O'Hara, who presently continues—

"But I myself was interviewed not long since."

"Indeed! On what subject, may I ask?"

"Well, I'll tell you how it was." And Mr. O'Hara finishes his grog. "A man in Killbeg—I found out afterwards that he was an Irish-American home on a visit —kept writing and writing to me, stating that he was the sole survivor from some deadly district, and wanted to tell me all about it, if I would only just grant him one single interview, just to ease his mind of the terrible burthen, which, he wrote, was slowly dragging him to an early grave. Well, Mr. Dolan, I never encourage stragglers at my office, because I want to get through my work as fast as I possibly can, but this man kept pestering me so much, and thinking that there might be half a column got out of him, I at length wrote inviting him to call at the office on a certain day, and at a certain hour. Well, sur, the hour came, and the man came with it—a tall, thin, consumptive-looking man he was, and fairly respectable in dress and manner. I motioned him to a chair, which he sank into with a weary sigh.

"'Now, sur,' I said briskly, 'you wish to give me some information regarding an extremely pestiferous district, from which, I have gathered through your numerous letters, you are the solitary survivor.'

"'Yes,' he answered, in a slow, shy voice. 'I thought that if the matter was ventilated through the medium of your powerful organ, something might perhaps be done.'

"'Done?'

"'Yes,' continued the stranger—'some meetings organized in the market-place, with a band and fireworks, just to entice the populace. This might lead to several questions being put to the Speaker in the House of Commons.'

"'Yes, yes,' I said impatiently; 'but to your story. Where is this deadly district?'

"'Not more than within a few dozen miles of Tipperary—a place called Ballymulgullian.'

"'And what brought you there?' I asked the man.

"'Ordered there by my doctor,' he answered. 'I'll tell you all about it. I had been for long years suffering from a complication of complaints, and this gradually brought on insomnious nights, loss of appetite, sudden blushing, shivering down the back, sense of fullness in the region of the stomach after meals, and so on. So the doctor ordered me to winter in Ballymulgullian, where he counted on the drowsy atmosphere and quietude of the locality wooing sleep to my weary eyes. Down I went, accompanied by a box of sleeping-draughts, which proved of the utmost value to my system, for the landlady came and woke me three times a night to take one. She was a treasure! But this is a digression. When I arrived in Ballymulgullian, it was to find it filled with a large draft of soldiers. When I quitted it, two months afterwards, half those soldiers were defunct, and the residue under marching orders for some less deadly locality.'

"'Half of them dead!' I exclaimed, preparing to take notes. 'Go on—tell me all about it.'

"'I am coming to it,' he answered. 'First the gallant colonel succumbed; then the major; then the noble captain; then the sergeant; next to shuffle off this mortal coil were the drum-major and two lance-corporals; then half the full privates followed their superior officers to the cold and silent grave.'

"'Good heavens!' I cried. 'What was the fell pestilence which carried them off in such appalling numbers? Was it typhoid?'

"'No,' said the man, beginning to weep.

"'Was it influenza?'

"'No.'

"'Small-pox?'

"'No; all the regiment had been only recently vaccinated.'

"'Well, what *was* the name of this awful plague?' I asked, pencil and book ready.

"'*Delirium tremens*,' sobbed the stranger."

As Mr. O'Hara repeats the last line he seizes the bottle, mixes himself some grog, drinks it, and then says—

"I declare to goodness, Mr. Dolan, I allowed that ruffian to leave my presence without kicking him downstairs!"

"I don't wonder at your forbearance," I answer after having a good laugh. "That man was a humourist of the deepest dye."

"That he was," Mr. O'Hara acknowledges; "but I wish he had gone somewhere else to exhibit his gift. I never felt so sore at being *done* in my life. I never saw the chap since—he is long since gone back to America. But if ever I drop on him, I'll give him Ta-ra-ra-boom-de-ay."

\* \* \* \* \*

During dinner Mr. O'Hara asks—

"Are you fond of racing, Mr. Dolan?"

"Oh, yes—what Irishman is not?"

"Then if you are here in another

month, you'll see some of the best hurdle-racing in Ireland."

"Indeed!" I say in surprise. "Where?"

"Why between here and Ballyboyle—just half-way—lies the racecourse. Have you never heard tell of the Mullinbeg Hurdle Races?"

"Oh, yes, to be sure!" I exclaim. "I remember now. And so they come off in a month's time?"

"Yes," says Mr. O'Hara. "I suppose you are not an owner?"

"No, though one of my best friends owns a fair string of horses."

"Is that so, Mr Dolan? Now, I'll tell you what you ought to do. Get your friend to bring over a couple of his horses, and enter them for one or two of our races."

"Ah, my dear boy, that's easier said than done," I tell him. "My friend is one of those rabidly anti-Irish men, and I don't believe the wealth of India would tempt him across St. George's Channel. And besides, you forget that his horses are flat-racers."

"Well, and what matter for that?" asks Mr. O'Hara. "There are two flat-races on the card each day, and if your friend's horses are any good at all, they could beat our lot without much trouble. We are not great in the flat-racing line in Ireland, as you know. The jumping sport is our crack game."

"Yes, Ireland was always a famous jumping country."

"Of course it was," says Mr. O'Hara, "of course it was. So, Mr. Dolan, take my advice, and write to your friend. Sure, wouldn't it be an act of charity to bring him here, and to let him see Ireland with his own eyes? I'll bet a new shilling he wouldn't return to England so anti-Irish as when he left it."

"I'm quite sure of that," I say.

"Of course you are," continues Mr. O'Hara. "And by the same token, he would not be the only English owner on the course. The chief event—called The County Cup—is bringing over one of the crack jumpers from the other side, and the Liverpool contingent always musters strong. They can cross by boat to Killbeg for seven shillings return, and the fare from there to Ballyboyle is only one-and-sixpence second class."

Mr. O'Hara apparently considers that nobody would think of travelling from Killbeg to Ballyboyle by any other than second-class.

"Well, I'll consider the matter," I say. "Though I fear it is useless writing to my friend."

"Never mind—just try him," is Mr. O'Hara's advice.

Coming on to nine o'clock he prepares to depart. Bartle wants him to drive back, but he will not hear of such a proposal.

"The night is far too fine and bright to waste on a car, Bartle," he says. "I'll walk it back to Ballyboyle. Will you come a bit of the way with me, Mr. Dolan?"

"By all means," I answer, putting on my hat.

The moon lights us along the straight white road, and the air is so still that the ghostly trees which stand sentinel along our route give never a whisper. Now and again the distant bay of a farmhouse dog, the sharp bark of the fox at play, or the melancholy moo of a lovesick cow, strikes on our ears, but no other sound disturbs night's reign.

"This is what we call a fairy's night

hereabouts," Mr. O'Hara presently informs me. "Bright and silent, and with never a breath of air. It appears that the 'good people' don't like windy nights—it being only witches that take delight in storms."

"I suppose, according to local belief, there are plenty of fairies about here?"

"Fairies!" echoes Mr. O'Hara. "Why, man dear, we could supply all the pantomimes in London next Christmas, and then have enough left to go on with. It's the divil's own place for fairies, and no mistake."

And here Mr. O'Hara lights his pipe, and begins a long tale concerning the doings of some of the local "good people," which tale lasts until we reach the milestone.

"Hold!" I cry. "I go no further."

"Very well, Mr. Dolan; now, won't you drop over on Friday to dinner?"

"I shall."

"That's the style—come to the office—say about four."

"All right; good-night."

"Good-night, Mr. Dolan — mind the fairies on your way back."

As I walk slowly homeward, my thoughts revert to the Alice mystery. What could the poor girl have been arrested for? How did Watts discover her? Was it by chance? I incline to the belief that it was, for I remember his start on first seeing her. This fact only makes the mystery deeper still. I wonder shall I ever come to know all about the business? Who knows?

With these thoughts wandering through my brain I reach the mill, and enter the narrow path between two thorn hedges, which leads from the bridge to the mill-house door. I am half-way through it when a man passes me, giving me a sharp, scrutinizing glance. Even in the moonlight I notice his fierce dark eyes and sallow cheeks. He passes swiftly on, and is soon lost to view. One of the peasantry, I could tell; but what fierce eyes the fellow had!

## CHAPTER VIII.

### A MOST MYSTERIOUS OUTRAGE.

FRIDAY evening finds me seated in the office of the *Ballyboyle Examiner,* a copy of which powerful organ I glance over, while its efficient and trenchant Editor—with a big E—corrects some proofs. That business being over, he hands the slips to an inky-faced, curly-headed "devil," and then turning to me, says—

"Now, Mr. Dolan, I am at your service."

Leaving the office, we walk for some length down the High Street, then turn to the left up a narrow road, and in a few minutes come to a trim little cottage, with its front garden enclosed by green palings and a rustic gate. Three Irish terriers greet their master with alternate wriggles and barks; then they each in turn have a sniff at my ankles, and on assuring themselves that I am not here for purposes of petty larceny, allow me to pass into the hall unmolested. The sitting-room is neatly furnished, and boasts a cottage piano. The table is "laid" for dinner, and has for a centre-piece a big, suspicious-looking black bottle. This my host grasps, and pouring some of its contents into a tumbler, adds some water, and hands the mixture to me, preparatory to mixing some for himself.

"You'll find it all right," he says. "It's some of the *rale* Home Rule."

I have a drink, and then exclaim—

"Why, this is poteen!"

"Right you are, Mr. Dolan. Never paid duty in its natural life!"

"Where did you get it?"

And Mr. O'Hara, with a merry twinkle in his eye, answers—

"You must ask me another. Every

Christmas morning and St. Patrick's eve, Pat—my head cook and bottle-washer—finds a little keg of this stuff laid nice and easy outside the back door. How the divil it comes there no one knows."

"And I don't suppose any one wants to know."

"The divil a one."

Here Pat enters with a tray containing a good homely dinner of boiled mutton and turnips, augmented by "lashins iv praties." Pat is a study. His hair is red, his face is red, and his eyes are of a reddish-brown. He is in his shirt-sleeves, and wears a white apron. After drawing two chairs to the table, he asks—

"Do you want anything else, sur?"

"No, Pat," answers his master, "except some hot potatoes when you think we require them."

"Right, sur," and Pat walks to the door.

Here he stops short. "Oh, I forgot to mintion, sur, that Mrs. Mulligan called to know if you would be so kind as for to put the funeral in the paper. I towld her I'd mintion the matther to you at me earliest convanience, sur."

"Oh, yes, tell her I have done so—she will find it in to-morrow's issue," says my host, helping me to some mutton.

"She towld me to ax what you'd charge, sur," continues Pat.

"Nothing at all, tell her; sure, isn't it news? But if she ever thinks of getting married again, tell her I'll put the wedding in for five shillings, and give a list of the guests. And look here, Pat, be sure and tell her how inexpressibly sorry I was on hearing of her poor husband's death. Tell her I fairly broke down when penning the obituary notice—don't forget that word— obituary."

"Arrah, shure he was no loss!" exclaims Pat. "Shure he ust to dhrink like a fish, so he ust, an' bet her black an' blue many a time. Faith, she ought to offer up a prayer to the Blessed Vargin for riddin' her iv such a baste!"

"Oh, for the Lord's sake, don't mention that to her!" cries Mr. O'Hara. "She's a yearly subscriber, and pays in advance."

"But shure every wan in the parish knows about him batin' her," persists Pat.

"Yes, yes, but that's no reason why we should remind her of the occurrence. Now, Pat,"—here Mr. O'Hara smiles sweetly upon his man,—"when Mrs. Mulligan calls again, tell her what I have told you, and add, in your own inimitable way, that should she ever deign to enter the holy state of matrimony again, I will give a glowing account of the nuptial ceremony. And now you may go."

"Yis, sur," and Pat vanishes.

"And so your paper comes out to-morrow?" I say.

"Yes, at ten o'clock—a large edition."

"Larger than usual?"

"Yes, sur—almost double as large."

"Then I suppose there will be some extra news in it?"

"Rather," and Mr. O'Hara winks his eye. "My dear Mr. Dolan, I'm as glad as anything you are here this evening. Do you know why?"

"No—tell me."

"Well, I intend showing you some fun to-night—some real fun. But you must hold your whisht."

"All right."

"As I told you, our town is in the divil's own bad way, and wants a stir."

"Yes, I dare say it does."

"It does indeed, sur; a little excitement

—help yourself to another murphy—a little excitement would do it all the good in the world. Hand me your plate, shure there's nothing on it, man dear! Well, as I was saying, the soldiers are the boys to make things lively all round, and wake up trade, so we are going to try and have them with us again."

"And how are you going to do it?" I ask.

"You will see to-night, my dear sur."

After dinner Mr. O'Hara sits at the piano and plays some rattling Irish reels and jigs, finishing up with 'Let Erin Remember.' Then after a tumbler of punch he warbles 'Purty Molly Brannigan' and 'The Night before Larry was stretched.'

About ten o'clock we stroll leisurely towards the printing-office. The shops are all closed, and the absence of lamp-light makes the place look like a deserted village.

But there is light in the printing-office, and I wait outside while Mr. O'Hara goes in to correct a couple of proofs. When he rejoins me I ask—

"Are you gone to press yet?"

"No," he answers, "a column remains open."

"What for?"

"You'll know presently—but remember, you must hear, see, and say nothing."

"Make your mind easy on that score," I assure him.

Presently we turn up a narrow passage of Cimmerian darkness, at the top of which we emerge on to a field bounded on the right by a wall, which encloses the back gardens of some of the High Street houses. Along by this wall we walk, Mr. O'Hara leading the way. Suddenly some one comes forth from the gloom of the field and confronts us. It is Pat.

"Have you got it all right?" whispers Mr. O'Hara to him.

"Yis, sur—safe as a chapel," Pat whispers back, as he produces a large tin canister.

"How long is the fuse?" asks his master.

"Jist long enough to give us five minits' start, sur."

"All right—don't make a noise with the match."

"Niver fear, sur—I've got thim silent wans."

Here Mr. O'Hara takes the canister and places it by the corner of a large door in the wall.

"Now, Pat," he whispers, "the instant you light the fuse run like a redshank across the field and home by Murphy's Lane."

"Right you are, sur," answers his man.

"Now, follow me quick, Mr. Dolan!" And close behind my host do I walk back to the High Street.

"What door was that?" I ask him, when we have gained the street.

"Whisht! It is the door leading to the back garden of the police barracks."

"The devil it is!" I exclaim.

At this moment a loud explosion startles the slumbering inhabitants, and sets every dog barking for miles round.

"God bless my soul!" cries Mr. O'Hara. "What can that be? Something is blown up. Oh, the cursed wretches! Follow me to the barracks!"

Along the street he runs, I of course running behind him. By this time windows are all open, and white figures peer from them out into the startled night. Doors are thrown back, and men half-dressed, and wholly scared, rush forth, invoking the protection of all the saints in the calendar. When we reach the police barrack it is to find it deserted.

"Follow me!" cries Mr. O'Hara for the second time, as he makes his way round to the back garden, at the further end of which stands the entire "force," lamps in hand. A smell of powder pervades the damp night air; and there, lying on the ground, is the wooden door, very much shattered.

"Good heavens! what's this?" exclaims Mr. O'Hara, taking out his note-book. "Tell me all about it, sergeant."

"It's a terrible business, Mr. O'Hara," answers the sergeant; "an' it's the marcy iv Providence that we warrent all blew up!"

"Hold your lamp here, sergeant," says Mr. O'Hara. "Now go on while I write."

The worthy sergeant holds the lamp close to Mr. O'Hara, and begins his tale in very measured, official tones.

"At about half-a-past-tin, me an' Constable O'Reilly was thinkin' iv goin' to bed, all the rest iv us bein' there already, barrin' wan on duty——"

"The name of the man on duty?" asks Mr. O'Hara, busy writing.

"Constable Dunn," continues the sergeant. "Well, just as we wor in the act iv puttin' out the lights in the barrack-room, we wor both knocked out iv our standin' be a triminjus ixplosion proceedin' from the ind iv our back gardin. We both rushed to the spot at wanst, and wor horrified to discover the door in the wall blew complately off iv its hinges be some powerful ixplosive substince. I immadiatly summonsed all the min from their beds, an' we proceeded to invistigate the affair, an' wor continuin' to do so whin you cum up."

"Have you got a clue?" asks Mr. O'Hara.

"You can state, sur, that the poliss is very reticent consarnin' the probable perpetrators iv the outrage," answers the sergeant.

"Very good," says Mr. O'Hara, closing his book. "I must hurry back to the office now, and stop the press while I write a leader on this diabolical affair. I hope and trust, for the honour and good name of our town, that the foul fiends may be tracked to their hiding-place and dragged forth to justice."

"Amen!" says the sergeant.

Back again to the High Street do we make our way, to find it crowded with excited men and women, who besiege the "Edithor" with questions anent the mysterious outrage.

"Don't ask me—don't ask me!" he cries to all. "I am composing the article in my mind. You will see a full account in to-morrow's *Examiner*."

When we at last get inside the office, my friend leans against the wall and indulges in a half-minute's quiet laugh.

"Isn't this immense?" he cries.

"But what if they should suspect Pat?"

"Oh, the divil a suspect, Mr. Dolan! Now I must set to at a rousing article."

"Very well," I say, "I'll start for home."

"Home!" he echoes. "Won't you stop the night with me? I'll make a shake-down for you—or rather for myself, and you can have my bed——"

"Nonsense!" I cry; "I would not dream of allowing you to do such a thing. No, the walk back will do me good."

"Well, if you must go, you must!" he declares; "only I'd rather you stopped. Anyhow, I'll send you a copy of the paper to-morrow, giving my indignant sentiments on the late outrage."

"Yes, do."

And with a mutual "Good-night" and grasp of the hand we part.

## CHAPTER IX.

### LIZ AND SHAUN.

When I reached the mill-house last night I found Bartle waiting up for me.

"Lord save me sowl, Mr. Dolan!" he cried, "I thought you wor lost."

"No, Bartle; the fact is, an explosion occurred at the police barracks."

"An ixplosion, sur! The Lord have marcy on us! Was there any one hurted?" And Bartle looked positively frightened.

"No, thank goodness, no one was injured, but the police had a narrow escape."

"Oh dear, oh dear!" he cried; "I must go and tell herself."

And away he went to tell his wife all

about it. I was not long ere I got between the sheets, and slept like the proverbial top until eight o'clock this morning.

About three o'clock I stroll into the kitchen, which boasts a regular five-barred grate, a yellow-faced Dutch clock, a really valuable collection of old china on the dresser, and actually *four* different sized pots, not to mention two distinct kettles. Here, for the first time, I have the honour of beholding the "babby"—I have *heard* him often enough. He is a very small mite, so small, indeed, that I feel a sort of conviction stealing upon me that his internal arrangements must be all lungs. His head is covered with white down—*very* white; but then, his father is a miller.

But my eyes quickly wander from Master McBride to his nurse. She is a perfect specimen of an Irish beauty—tall, billowy-bosomed, with large deep, dark-blue eyes, and wavy hair with the well-known Irish purple gloss. She blushes and smiles on seeing my eyes fixed upon her, and turns to the door leading to the mill-yard. This door is open, and as she stands outside it, I can see through the window that a man has come up and is speaking to her. It is the man who passed me with such a fierce look the other night. It does not require the sound of his voice to tell me where he hails from. Those dark eyes, sallow cheeks, and raven locks proclaim the Galway man. Those eyes lose all their fierceness, and become beautifully soft and tender as he looks at the girl. Those sallow cheeks assume a warmer tinge when she looks at him.

"An' I suppose I can cum an' see you most ivery day, acushla?" he is saying.

"Arrah, I don't know at all, Shaun," the girl answers. "Shure, mebbe Mrs. McBride wouldn't like me to be always talkin' wid you."

"An' why not—eh?" he asks, with a momentary return of the old fierce look. "Why not, Liz?"

"Shure, she might be thinkin' I wasn't mindin' me work."

"Arrah, what work?" he demands. "Shure you don't call mindin' a babby work?"

"Oh, begorra I do!" and Liz laughs at him. "Musha, an' what do you know about the matther, Shaun?"

"The divil a much, agrah!" and Shaun smiles grimly. "Howsomdever, she can't mind me cummin wanst or twiste a week, so she can't."

"Musha, an' I don't know at all, Shaun."

At this point Mrs. McBride bustles into the kitchen, duster and besom in hand.

"An' is it here you are, sur!" she exclaims. "Shure the kitchen is terribly dirty, so it is! Won't you sit down, sur?" And she dusts a chair for me.

"I hope you don't mind my smoking here, Mrs. McBride?"

"Oh, the sorra a mind, sur; but, Lord save me, Mr. Dolan, you smoke a power! Shure it's not good for a young man, so it's not. Mind you, sur, I noticed for the last few days you're not yourself at all, at all."

"Nonsense, Mrs. McBride, I'm fit as a fiddle."

Here she goes to the door leading to the yard, and beholds Shaun and Liz, who have been silent since her advent to the kitchen.

"Now thin, Shaun Burk, what brings you gosterin' round my door?" she demands. "Jist take yourself on out iv this, an' don't be takin' up Liz's time. You lazy, idle shooler, why don't you go an' work?"

Here Liz turns back into the kitchen with downcast eyes, and stands with her back to me "huzzing" the baby.

"Answer me *that*, Shaun!" continues Mrs. McBride.

"Arrah, shure I'm goin' to," says Shaun, trying to stop frowning.

"You're goin' to!" echoes Mrs. McBride in scornful tones. "You're always goin' to, but the sorra a hapert you iver do! An' the idaya iv the likes iv you comin' hankerin' afthur the likes iv Liz! A purty boy she'd git! An' tell me *this*, Shaun Burk, what soort iv a husband would *you* make a dacent girl—eh?"

"Why, the right soort," answers Shaun, with darkened cheeks and gleaming eyes.

"The right soort!" And Mrs. McBride gives a contemptuous sniff. "Begorra, I'm afeered it would be a starvin' wife and family you'd be havin'! So be off wid you now, an' if I ketch you here agin I'll tell the min to sling you into the race."

Shaun, now pale with passion, is about to break forth in reply, but with a mighty effort he restrains himself, and putting his hands in his pockets, walks quickly away.

Mrs. McBride comes back into the kitchen, and after "tipping me a wink," turns to Liz.

"Now, you Liz," she says in very severe tones, "don't let me ketch yous two gosterin' together agin. The idaya iv a purty fine girl like you takin' up wid the like iv *that* soort iv a sloother! Arrah, where's your sinses?"

"Shure I don't want him to come afthur me at all, ma'am, so I don't," answers Liz, still with her back to us.

"Very well, thin—I'll show him to the differ if I ketch him comin' round any more wid his sleevien talk. So go on wid you now, an' walk up an' down the front door."

And without a word Liz leaves the kitchen.

"What an extremely handsome girl," I remark, when she is well out of hearing.

"Yes, sur, that she is." And the dear lady bestows a quick, penetrating glance upon me. "She is the purtiest girl in the county, an' that's sayin' sometin'. An' not a sowl has the crature belongin' to her in the whole worrld, barrin' an ould uncle who she was rale glad to git away from, for he's most always dhrunk—the baste! An' to think iv her takin' up wid the likes iv Shaun Burk!"

"I don't think she is *very* much in love with Shaun," I say—"so far as I can see."

"Mebbe you're right, sur; but shure, she darren't look at any wan else."

"How is that?"

"Bekaze Shaun would bate thim black an' blue. Shure, only last summer, a strong farmer from Cody's Cross, be the name of Pete Burn, kem coortin' her, but begorra, sur, Shaun met him goin' home wan night an' nearly murdered him!" And Mrs. McBride cannot help laughing at the thought of it. "Nearly murdered the poor man! An' Pete niver show'd his nose within the bawl iv an ass iv here, from that good day to this."

"That's a pity," I say. "Such a fine girl deserves a good husband."

"'Deed she does, sur—ivery wan notices her. Av coorse she hasn't the same soort iv fatures as Alice. Lord save me, Mr. Dolan, what's got Alice at all?"

"I really don't know, Mrs. McBride."

And so saying I rise and return to the sitting-room.

Seated by the window, I watch Liz as she paces to and fro outside. She is not long ere she is aware of my presence, and at once restricts her walk to the space opposite the window. Ah, Liz, I am afraid you are an over true daughter of Eve. But where is the serpent? Not in sight yet. However, I have just caught sight of the would-be avenger, whose sallow face and fierce eyes are even now concealed behind that hedge over there to the right, by the garden. Shaun, Shaun, beware of jealousy! *Liz loves you not.*

Oh, dear me! I begin to grow weary of this life here. What will I do? Leave for London—or wait for the races? Happy thought—write to Langton!

## CHAPTER X.

### THE CHRISTENING.

YESTERDAY evening I wrote and despatched the following note—

"*Tolka Mill,*
"*Near Ballyboyle, Ireland.*

"MY DEAR LANGTON,

"Notwithstanding your fierce anti-Irishism, I venture to inform you that there will be a two days' race meeting held near here next month, and as I happen to know something, I give you the tip that a couple of your horses would have a real good chance on both days.

"Besides all this, you would have the inestimable benefit of *my* society while here, not to mention your surprise and delight on seeing with your own eyes what this terrible country really is. So come along.

"Yours as ever,
"Arthur Dolan."

By the way, it was shortly after despatching the above that a copy of that powerful organ, the *Ballyboyle Examiner*, came to hand. On opening it I came upon the following article, in all the dignity of "leaded" type—

"DASTARDLY OUTRAGE LAST NIGHT.

"Last night, at the hour of half-past ten, our quiet town was suddenly startled from its dreamy slumber by an appalling explosion, which shook the trembling earth for miles round. In an incredibly short space of time the streets were alive with a terrified, indignant, and partly-dressed populace, who fearfully asked one another if the Day of Judgment had arrived. Our reporter was quickly upon the scene, and his luminous description of the affair will be found in another portion of our paper. From its perusal it will be gathered that the explosion occurred at the door leading from the back garden of the constabulary barracks to O'Farrell's field, which door—a massive wooden structure—was completely wrecked by the agency of some powerful explosive—possibly dynamite. Fortunately the wall itself was not seriously damaged. It can be seen at a glance that a most dastardly, deadly, and diabolical outrage has been perpetrated, and it is only by a superhuman miracle that the entire barracks, with its valuable contents—six constables and a sergeant—have not been blown into empty space! What an appalling picture to contemplate, even in our mind's eye, as the Swan of Avon says. The valuable lives of six constables and a sergeant sacrificed to the devilish designs of a gang of machinating miscreants dwelling within our midst!

"Now we ask—ask calmly, dispassionately, and with the entire voice of Ballyboyle and the surrounding country—how much longer will the English Government leave our town unprotected? Ballyboyle, the centre of the commercial and agricultural prosperity of the whole county! How long is Ballyboyle to patiently submit to the degradation of an empty military barracks? We pause for a reply, amid the smoking ruins of the shattered door. We counsel our fellow-citizens to calmness in this crisis. We conjure them to avoid all mischievous agitations, which would only defeat their own object. Our demands are just, and must be complied with."

Wonderful man, O'Hara! What a fortune he would be to a London halfpenny evening paper, with aspirations!

After dinner this evening Mrs. McBride enters with a serio-comic look, and a small tray containing a glass of very dark port, and a plate, upon which lies a thick slab of some mahogany-looking substance, to one end of which adheres about an inch of what I take to be plaster-of-Paris.

"Mr. Dolan," she says, placing the tray on the table, "the babby was christened to-day."

"Oh, indeed! I hope he behaved himself during the performance."

"Bedad he did, sur—niver cried wanst. Now I've took the liberty iv bringing you a drop iv port wine, an' a slice iv the christenin' cake, for to wish health an' long life to Patrick Bartle McBride, sur."

"It was really very kind of you to think of me, Mrs. McBride, and I have great pleasure in drinking long life to your son."

Here I seize that glass of port, and drink it off in one desperate draught. Then, on my promising to attack the cake "presently,"

Mrs. McBride leaves me to myself, having done her best to poison me. What am I to do with this awful slice of cake? I have it! That choleric gander, who is leading his harem in a walk along the race, has on several occasions endeavoured to nip me by the ankle. The brute is as fierce as a cock ostrich. But he is not a cock ostrich, and so I will give him this slice of cake.

About half-past nine I hear sounds of revelry proceeding from the kitchen, so decide upon having a peep at the christening party. Accordingly I slip round to the yard, and take up my position outside the kitchen window—not too close to it, for should any of the guests catch sight of me, the whisper would go round, and half the fun would be spoiled.

Bartle is dressed in his "Sunday best," and is quite innocent of flour, save about the head, where it seems to have taken root for ever. Mrs. McBride is apparelled in a gorgeous blue silk dress, but has been careful to supplement it by a large black apron. The guests—all in their Sunday clothes, you may be sure—number a round dozen, and are seated close to the wall, leaving the centre of the floor clear. On a table by the window is a jar of whisky, a decanter of port—*that* port—(for the ladies), and any amount of glasses. On another table, in one of the corners, is the remains of the christening cake—*that* cake. It possesses awful powers of fascination over Mick's son —I mean the genius whose profound researches in the natural history of cats so astonished his father, and, I may add, myself. There he sits in his little corduroy jacket, with bright brass buttons, tweed trousers, clogs, and shock-head, his eyes firmly riveted on that fearful compound. I suppose he has eaten about three pounds of it already, and he still not only lives, but is ready for another pound. These are the sort of stomachs we have to deal with in Ireland. Let the English Government look to it!

Mick is also present, of course, with his wife, a thin, delicate-looking woman. Three more of the miller's men grace the room, with their sweethearts—fine, buxom girls, with rosy cheeks and flashing teeth. In a corner of the fireplace sits Liz nursing Master Patrick, who seems to be asleep. Many are the stolen glances in her direction from the boys, but, for once, she does not appear to notice them, and seems shy and nervous. Seated with his back to the fireplace is the old blind fiddler, who is now engaged in playing 'The Angel's Whisper,' and very well he plays it. When he has finished Bartle rises and brings him a glass of whisky, which he drinks in one draught.

And now one of the "boys" begins singing 'The Rising of the Moon,' the chorus of which is taken up by the whole company. This proves a little too much for Master Patrick Bartle McBride. With a yell which rings clear and loud over the united voices of the company, he announces his disapprobation; and though the singing is stopped immediately, he continues to yell so fearfully that Liz has to carry him out of the kitchen.

"Now, Andy, begin it agin," says Bartle. "Shure the little divil has no taste for music."

And Andy begins again, and the whole song, chorus and all, is gone through with great applause. Then Mick is called upon to oblige.

"Shure I don't railly know anything," he declares. But the company one and all exclaim, "That'll do you now!" Whereupon

Mick grins, scratches the back of his head, and forthwith begins the 'Whistling Thief,' in the course of which celebrated song his imitations of the pig grunting, the dog barking, and all the rest of the traditional "business," makes all the company nearly die with laughter.

After the song there is a great run on the whisky and port, while the company fall into detached conversation. At this juncture Mrs. McBride calls Liz, who reappears with Master McBride asleep in her arms. She sits down in the corner, and her mistress brings her a glass of wine.

"Now, Liz, alanna, we want to hear you sing," cries Bartle.

Liz blushes deep crimson, and holds down her face to the baby.

"Yis, Liz," adds Mrs. McBride. "Shure we all know what a sweet lilt you can give."

"Ay, that we do!" from the boys.

Mrs. McBride takes the baby from the girl, saying,

"Now, Liz, don't be bashful."

And Liz, after a pause, begins the 'Coolin.' Her voice is wonderfully sweet—sweet enough to lure some one out of the shadows of the night; some one who has been watching the window from a distance. He now stands right beside me, scarcely noticing my presence, as with glistening eyes and smiling lips he drinks in the music. So he stands until Liz concludes, and then he sinks back into the night once more.

What a mighty power must Love possess, when it can transform a face of wild fierceness to one of almost womanly tenderness at the sound of a girl's voice!

Presently the fiddler starts a jig, the younger members of the company "take the floor," and so I leave them.

Poor Shaun! He still remains under cover of the darkness, watching the window from a distance. I pass him as I leave the yard to return to the sitting-room *viâ* the front door. Mrs. McBride *might* have asked him to the christening—just for *wanst*. A thought strikes me, and I return to where he stands.

"You seem to have been left out in the cold?" I say.

"Ah no, sur," he replies; "I'm right enough, so I am."

"Will you come round to the front door and have a glass of whisky?"

He does not answer, but directs his glance towards the window.

"Come along," I say. "You can come back here again."

With a "Thank you, sur," he accompanies me round to the front door.

"Come inside," I say.

"Ah no, sur—shure I'm forbid the house. I'd rayther stop where I am."

"Very well. I will be with you in a minute."

I go to the sitting-room, mix a stiff glass of grog, and then ring the bell. It is quickly answered by Liz.

"Liz, bring this to the person standing at the hall-door," I say, handing her the tumbler.

"Yis, sur," she answers, taking the tumbler, and looking a little surprised as she leaves with it.

It is not long ere I hear her shutting the door; but instead of coming back to the room with the tumbler, she leaves it on the hall-table, and returns to the kitchen.

Well, the poor devil has been able to speak to her, any way!

## CHAPTER XI.

#### THE RESULTS OF NIGHT SHOOTING.

To my very great surprise and pleasure, I received the following letter by this morning's post—

"*Olympic Club,*
"*London, W.*

"My dear Arthur,

"Your welcome letter reached me in due course. I think your advice about running a couple of my horses at your local meeting a capital one, and have given instructions to Jones to get Madge into trim for the event. (I have re-christened the Vixen, Madge, as I did not like the former name.) I will write to the Secretary of the Ballyboyle Hunt Committee—he, according to the advertisement, being also secretary of the Mullinbeg Race Committee

—and enter Madge for a race on each of the days. Look out for a stable, and write when you have secured one. Also try and secure me a bed in your old mill—if it be only in the wheel! Hoping you are fit,

    "I remain, yours sincerely,
        "JOHN LANGTON."

A miracle has come to pass in this prosaic *fin de siècle*. Langton is actually coming to Ireland! I scarcely hoped that he would even send one of his horses over. How glad I am to know that he will soon be here! To tell the truth, I was beginning to grow very lonely and restless.

I have given the trout a two days' respite, nor do I care to tempt them even this choice angler's afternoon. No, I will not fish, I will stroll by the river-bank and muse. Musing is not a good habit in a young man, I admit, unless he be of a poetic temperament, in which case the more he muses (if it keeps him from writing) the better.

I have not strolled very far along the bank ere I come upon Mr. O'Hara in the act of landing a very fine trout.

"Here you are!" I exclaim. "Now, why the deuce didn't you let us know you were here?"

"Oh, I don't like bothering people," he answers. "And how are you, Mr. Dolan— all right, eh?"

"Ripping!"

"That's all right! Well, I'll just go over with you now, and sample your grog —just to show there's no ill-feeling."

"That's the style," I say. "I'm so glad I met you. I was beginning to feel a regular hermit."

"Ah, it's bad to live too much alone," declares Mr. O'Hara. "Why don't you get married, Mr. Dolan? It would be a little excitement for you."

"I dare say it would," I answer, laughing. "But I must find Mrs. Right first. Talking of excitement, have you got the military in Ballyboyle yet?"

"No," he answers, laughing quietly; "but they are busy considering the matter in the Castle. We must give them another outrage."

"How?" I ask.

"I don't exactly know at present; but my fertile brain is at work, and you will hear of some fresh and startling occurrence before the week is out."

When we reach the house, we find Liz seated outside the window nursing the baby.

"An' is it here I find you, Liz, my darling?" asks Mr. O'Hara. "Not married yet!"

Liz only blushes and smiles in reply, and Mr. O'Hara continues—

"Well, well; what are all the boys about? That's what I want to know. The idea of such a fine girl as yourself going about without a husband! Where's Shaun?"

"I don't know, sur," Liz answers, keeping her eyes fixed on Master Patrick.

"Oh, I suspect he is not far away," I say, and we both pass into the house.

\* \* \* \* \*

Mr. O'Hara has remained for dinner, and now in the cool twilight we are both seated outside the window enjoying a post-prandial whiff. Presently the miller joins us. It can be easily seen that he has a grievance.

"What's the matter with you, Bartle?" asks Mr. O'Hara. "You're not in your usual form this evening."

"Faith, I'm not," Bartle declares. "Not be no manner iv manes."

"What's wrong?" I ask him.

"There is a divil iv a hawk mozieng about this mill," he explains; "an' he's robbin' herself's chickens right an' lift, bad luck to him! I'd like to shoot his skull aff iv him. Be cripes, I would!"

"Where does he rest?" Mr. O'Hara wants to know.

"Beyant in thim trees be the road, dang his skin! Only this mornin' he swoops down, me dear, an' walks off in the wink iv an eye wid a lovely fine chicken—the thief iv the world!"

"Have you got a gun?" asks Mr. O'Hara.

"The divil a wan, sur—only an ould blunderbuss."

"Have you any powder and shot?"

"Lashins, sur!"

"Is the bluderbuss safe?"

"Safe as a chapel!" Bartle exclaims. "A dale safer thin thim newfangled brach-loaders. Yarrah, man dear, shure its barrel is as thick as a cannon!"

"Then bring it here, and we'll load it, and have a shot at the robber."

"Right you are, sur," cries Bartle, turning to enter the house. But he suddenly pauses and continues—"Howld on though, Mr. O'Hara—shure I have no licence for shootin'."

"Hang the matter!" answers the Editor. "Who is going to see us? And if any one hears the report, how will they know who pulled the trigger?"

"Thrue for you, sur," says Bartle; and away he goes to get the weapon, while my guest and I return to the sitting-room, where the candles are now alight.

Presently Bartle comes in bearing the

blunderbuss, and we find that he has treasured it with loving care. It is as clean, polished, and bright as on the day it was purchased.

"Begad, Bartle, you ought to get six months on the plank-bed for harbouring such a deadly-looking object as this!" says Mr. O'Hara, taking the piece, and critically examining it. "Why, nothing would be safe within a radius of fifty yards when this went off!"

Here he cocks the big hammer, and pulling the trigger, down it snaps on the black flint, emitting a regular *feu de joie*.

"Yow!" exclaims Bartle. "That's a rale Home Rule touch!"

"Where did you get it?" I ask him.

"It was prisinted to me gran'father, sur, be owld Lord Crogan. An' from that very windy there behind you, me gran'father blew the skull aff iv a Whiteboy wid it."

"Faith, I'm not surprised at that," says Mr. O'Hara. "It would nearly hold a quart of shot!"

"Bedad, he did so," continues the miller. "Blew the skull complately aff iv him—the Lord have marcy on his sowl!"

"Now, Bartle, where's the powder and shot?" queries the Editor.

"Oh, bedambut, I clane forgot thim!" answers Bartle. "Wait a moment, sur; I'll be back wid thim in a shout."

He hurries away, and returns in a few minutes with a powder-flask and shot-pouch, which he hands to Mr. O'Hara, who forthwith begins loading the blunderbuss, using paper for wadding, there being nothing else handy.

"Now come along," he says.

Out we sally, and make our way down the path by the top of the garden, until we come to the hedge which runs along by the road, and which is backed by a line of tall elms.

"Now I'll walk in front," says Mr. O'Hara, "just for fear of accidents. You two keep close behind me, and sling a couple of stones into each tree we come to."

There are plenty of stones at our feet, so Bartle and I fill our pockets, and then we start in quest of the hawk.

Tree after tree do we pass, landing stones into each. So intent are we that we fail to hear the sound of approaching wheels on the road. It is only when the car is abreast of us that we notice it. So does the hawk, and forth he flutters from the tree. There is an awful report from that blunderbuss, followed by a shout of terror from the road, as the car breaks into lightning speed, and is soon out of hearing.

"Holy Moses, you've shot some wan!" cries Bartle.

"The divil a shoot!" answers Mr. O'Hara, "unless the 'some one' was up in the air! But I have succeeded in frightening the life out of some one on a car. Here, run home like the mischief, and hide this deadly weapon, together with the powder and shot. And remember—you know nothing."

"Bedambut, you may take your oath on *that!*" answers Bartle, taking the blunderbuss, and running homewards with it as fast as he can go.

"I hope you have not peppered anybody," I say.

"Not at all," replies the Editor, laughing; "I fired up in the air. But the occupant of that car will swear he was fired at."

"Will there be a stir about it?"

"Rather?"

"In what way?"

"Why, whoever the fellow was will be

sure to give information to the police, and from them the matter will come to the knowledge of the press—the press, sur!" and the Editor chuckles.

"And what then?" I ask.

"What then? Why, I will have a long article on this, the second outrage within a fortnight in our county, and will once more demand the presence of military. It is the luckiest thing that ever occurred!"

Within another hour Mr. O'Hara is on his way home to Ballyboyle, congratulating himself on the splendid materials which he possesses for the concoction of a "wake-them-up" article. It is a regular sin that such a journalistic genius should be wasting his "copy" on the Ballyboyle air—no, *Ballyboyle Examiner* I should have said.

## CHAPTER XII.

### LANGTON ARRIVES.

As I crossed the mill-yard a couple of days ago, I caught sight of Bartle through one of the doors of the stable, as he was busy directing some men who were working hard with brush and pail. All at once the dire thought that I had never looked out for a stable for Madge flashed upon me!

"What are you so busy with the stables for?" I asked, entering the door.

"Oh, begorra, shure I must have thim ready for the races, sur," Bartle replied. "Av coorse, I always have at laste two horses here during the racin'. You see, it is handy to the coorse."

"Yes, Bartle, and I am thanking my stars that I have noticed you here."

"Arrah, why, sur?"

"Because a friend of mine wants a stall for a horse which he is bringing over for the races."

"Lord save me sowl, is that a fact?" cried Bartle.

"A solemn fact, I assure you."

"Ah, thin, with the help iv God, Mr. Dolan, you'll have the best box in this stable."

I thanked him, and then sought Mrs. McBride, to ask her to prepare a bedroom. This business being accomplished, I wired result to Langton.

As I did not expect him for at least a week, what was my surprise and pleasure on his advent this morning!

"What, Langton!" I cried. "You dear old chappie, why, I did not hope to see you for another week! This is a joyous surprise!"

"I'm glad to hear you say so, Arthur!" he answered. "Fact is, I felt in the blues, and so determined on coming over to bore you."

He had nothing but pæans of praise for the railway accommodation, the speed of the trains (ye gods!), and the general faultless efficiency of everything and everybody he had met with since he landed in Ireland. *Could* this be Langton?

He came in to luncheon, humming 'St. Patrick's Day,' and declared that the Irish climate was the most equable in the world.

"Why, Langton," I said at length, "what has come over you? Once upon a time you were the most truly anti-Irish beggar on the face of the earth."

"Ah, that was my ignorance, my dear

boy! If you want to know a country you must visit it."

"Yes, but you have not been here for five minutes yet!"

"I have been here long enough, my dear Arthur, to become fully aware that my former opinions were the result of ignorance and British bigotry."

Langton is about forty-five, smooth-faced, and with light-brown hair and clear blue eyes. He owns a small property near Brighton, and is a thorough sportsman of the old school—never betting (except it be a new hat) on any race.

Luncheon being over, we sit chatting over "things in general." Presently he says—

"By the way, Arthur, do you know that fellow, Captain Tempest?"

"I have heard of him—you mean the racing man?"

"Yes; he is coming over with his crack hurdle-racer, the Shah, for the big race here."

" Never ! "

" Fact."

" What sort of a chap is he ? "

" Well, to tell you the truth, Arthur, I don't like the fellow. I don't know why—he is always very civil. I suppose it is my bigoted nature again."

" What is he captain in ? "

"Oh, 'Captain Tempest' is only his racing name. I *did* hear his real name, but forget it. No, I *don't* like the beggar. There is a sort of lurking devil in his eye, with all his polite, civil ways. He reminds me of a fellow I once read of in some novel—a sort of chap who took the most fiendish pleasure in doing things to annoy others. You know the sort of character."

"And so he is bringing over his crack to Mullinbeg?"

"Yes; and oddly enough, he asked me where I was going to put up; and when I told him I was going to stay at a place called the 'Tolka Mill,' he seemed to be grinning — actually grinning, confound him!"

"I suppose he was amused at the notion of your stopping at a mill," I say.

"I don't know so much about that!" Langton continues. "On my saying that the fishing was reported to be good here, he remarked that he would most likely come and see if the report was correct while in Ireland."

"Well, if he does come, it will be so much the better for Mrs. McBride," I say. "The more guests the merrier is *her* motto."

By and by we go for a stroll by the river. As we leave the house we meet Liz with the baby, and the old smile and blush come to her face on seeing Langton gazing upon her with admiring eyes.

"Bless my soul! what a splendid-looking creature!" he remarks, as we walk on.

"Yes," I say; "and you should see the fierce-looking swain she has. It is as much as your life is worth to look at her in his presence."

"Ah, that shows how true his love is, Arthur. Don't you know what English women say? They say that Irishmen make the best husbands."

"And you agree with that sentiment, Jack?"

"Certainly I do," he replies emphatically. "And moreover, I am quite sure that Irish women make the best wives."

"Jack, Jack!" I exclaim with a laugh. "What the deuce *has* come over you?"

And I solemnly declare that the man

actually blushes! Ho! ho! I begin to suspect the truth. If there is not a woman at the bottom of all this, I am a Dutchman! However, I will hear, see, and say nothing for the present. Now he asks in a casual way—

"Do you know many of the county families round here?"

"I know none of them," I tell him.

"Why, how is that?" he queries, looking at me in surprise, mingled, I fancy, with a trace of disappointment.

"How is it? Well, that's easily explained," I say. "I do not belong to this part of Ireland. Were I in my native district I could introduce you into every house worth entering. But down here I am a stranger, not having sought any local society."

After walking along in silence for a while, he suddenly inquires—

"Is there not some place about here called Grange Foyle?"

"Grange Foyle? Oh, yes, I believe there is such a place somewhere near here. Why do you ask?"

"Oh, I have heard of such a place."

"When?"

"Some time ago," he answers quickly.

"But have you heard anything particular about it?"

"Oh no, not at all." And he relapses into silence again.

Yes, the magnet that has attracted John Langton to Ireland is to be found in Grange Foyle. Wonder who she is? Bartle, his wife, or O'Hara, will no doubt be able to give me the information.

"By the way, Langton, what about Madge?"

He starts, flushes slightly, and echoes, "Madge!"

"Yes, when is she coming over? the stable is ready."

"Oh, to be sure, to be sure!" he exclaims. "She, with her jockey, will arrive here two days before the race."

"Who is her jockey?"

"White."

"A good man—a very good man," I say.

We return to the house after an hour's walk.

Ten to one on the magnet's name being *Madge!*

## CHAPTER XIII.

### LANGTON'S FATE.

YESTERDAY morning a copy of the *Ballyboyle Examiner* came to hand, containing the following very important article—

### "MURDEROUS OUTRAGE.

A LANDLORD FIRED ON!

*What is our Country coming to?*

"We print in another portion of this paper a letter from Sir James O'Tyrrell, Bart., copied from the London *Times*. Its perusal will bring the blush of heart-stricken grief and shame to thousands of manly brows. It will be gathered from its contents, that as Sir James was driving in his private car from Ballyboyle to his noble and ancestral seat at Ennistyrrell, on the night of the 18th instant, he was deliberately fired upon from behind a hedge by some murderous assassins, but, thank Heavens! most miraculously escaped uninjured. Again, and for the last time, we inquire—*What are the Castle authorities thinking of?* This is not a time for mincing words. We boldly declare that the infamous, dastardly, and cowardly nincompoopery betrayed by the Castle hirelings is looked upon with loathing by the entire civilized world. It is little more than two weeks ago since our town was rudely shaken to its heart's core by an appalling explosion, which was within an ace of blowing our whole police barracks into empty space. And hardly has the smoke cleared into the eternal welkin, scarcely have the last faint echoes of the thunder died away on the distant hills, ere one of our oldest patricians, one of our most popular landlords, a kind friend, a tender husband, an indulgent father, and a good Catholic, is wantonly fired upon by midnight murderers. What answer will our bungling, blundering brotherhood of officialdom make to this latest outcome of their devilish dilatoriness? Will they remain in a lethargic, comatous state until our town is in flames, our women and children murdered in cold blood, and our husbands, fathers, and brothers left lamenting their cursed fate? MILITARY! MILITARY! we call for, nay, DEMAND, in the name of IRISH MANHOOD. We will say no more."

Wonderful man! *O'Hara-go-Bragh!* should be the watchword of Ballyboyle. That reminds me, the trenchant Editor intimated that he would most likely be found by the Tolka to-day, so I will e'en go and hunt him up, Langton having driven over to the Race Committee Rooms. I find the great man sitting on the bank arranging his tackle.

"Well, O'Hara, I have read your eye-opener; any military yet?"

"Next week—next week," he answers, laughing.

"Is that so?"

"To be sure it is! My dear sur, the *Ballyboyle Examiner* is a great institution. But how the devil are you? I was just thinking of going over and having a glass of grog with you."

"Well, come along," I say, "I came over here with the express purpose of marching you back with me."

He quickly rises, and accompanies me back to the house, and down we sit to luncheon.

In the midst of our conversation Bartle

appears with an open letter, and a very mystified look.

"Is that for me, Bartle?"

"No, sur—it cum to me, all the way from London."

"Indeed! Who sent it?"

"Wan Captin Timpist."

"Tempest?"

"Yis, sur; he wants a room to be got ready for him for the races."

"Well, can he have it?"

"Oh yis, sur—but how the divil he cum to find out the place, an' we not advertisin' now, bates all!" and Bartle scratches a cloud of flour from the back of his head.

"I think I can explain that," I tell him. "Captain Tempest is an acquaintance of Mr. Langton's, who possibly told him of this place."

"Arrah, *now* I see it!" and Bartle brightens up at having the puzzle explained to him. "Well, we will make him as snug as we can, sur, you may be shure."

"How is the hawk getting on, Bartle?" asks Mr. O'Hara.

"The sorra a light or sight I've seen iv him iver sense, sur," answers the miller. "You must have kilt him."

"No, I don't think so," says the Editor. "If I hit him you would have been sure to find him before this."

"Arrah, how could I, sur?" cries Bartle. "Shure if you shot him at all you must have blew him into nothin'!"

"Ah, I forgot that." And on this confession from the Editor Bartle leaves us.

"Well, the idea of Tempest coming to stay here!" I say, half to myself.

"Is he a friend of yours?" asks Mr. O'Hara.

"No, I have never met him. By the

way, I suppose this meeting will be very successful."

"Rather! Why, Mr. Dolan, it will do your eyes good to see the grand stand! It will be as full as a barrel of herrings with all the best people in the county, not to mention the visitors from the other side of the Channel."

"Ah, that reminds me—do you know a place called Grange Foyle near here?"

"Do I not!" answers Mr. O'Hara. "Why, it is the finest place in the county. And, moreover, Mrs. Desmond is a model agent, and all the tenants swear by her. The rents come in as regular as the tide in Killbeg Bay. Sure, isn't this mill part of the property—come through an uncle, Lord Crogan."

"But who is this Mrs. Desmond, and who is she agent for?"

"For her cousin, Miss Ethel Foyle, who

is travelling abroad with her aunt. You see the property was left by Lord Crogan to Ethel, who was only a little girl at the time, so Mrs. Desmond, her cousin, became her agent—at least Mrs. Desmond's husband did, until his death."

"Oh, then Mrs. Desmond is a widow?"

"Why, of course she is, and the finest woman in Ireland—and that's saying something!"

"You don't say so?" I say, now divining that I am on the track of Langton's Fate.

"Yes, sur," continues Mr. O'Hara, warming with his subject. "Why, half the men in the county have proposed to her."

"Is that so?"

"Yes—she's a darling, that's what she is!" and Mr. O'Hara hides his emotion in his tumbler.

"I suppose she often goes to London?"

"Yes, every May; but she always comes

back for the races, when she has a houseful of guests. But talking of guests, Mr. Dolan, when are you coming to dine with me again? Come over some day, and I'll give you a song and a jig on the piano."

"Also an explosion?"

"No, no more explosions, or outrages of any kind, unless the military fail to put in an appearance," he answers, laughing. "So make up your mind, and come over next week."

"All right," I say; "I'll storm your castle in due time."

"That's the style. And now I must leave you alone in your glory. I've got a lot of work to do to-night." And in another five minutes he is on his way back to Ballyboyle.

N.B.—The magnet's name is Madge Desmond.

## CHAPTER XIV.

### MY FATE.

YESTERDAY brought a telegram from Langton's trainer announcing that Madge had pulled up lame after her morning spin.

"Confound it!" cried Langton, throwing down the message in disgust. "Isn't this too bad?"

"Any chance of running a stable companion?" I asked.

"None whatever—the entries are published. I'm right down wild, Arthur! What's to be done?"

"Go over at once and see how she is. Perhaps things are not so serious after all. Start at once; the midday train will land you in Dublin in ample time to catch the mail from Kingstown."

"Hanged if I don't take your advice, Arthur!"

And he did. By this time he has reached the trainer's.

I have been after the trout all the morning, and am returning to the house, when, passing the kitchen-door—which stands open—I meet Master Patsey O'Brien.

"Well, Patsey, have you discovered anything further concerning cats?"

"No, sur," he answers gravely; "nothin' more."

"And have you thought of writing on any other subject?"

"Oh yes, sur," and he brightens up. "I have writ a lesson on polismin."

"On policemen?"

"Yes, sur."

"I should very much like to see it, Patsey."

"Shure I have it in me pocket, sur." And putting his hand into his trousers pocket, he pulls forth a roll of foolscap. "Here it is, sur—writ all be meself wid a pin an' ink out iv me own head." And with a flush of pride he hands me the essay.

I unfold it, and read it aloud. It is written as follows, the punctuation alone being supplied by me—

"POLISMIN.

"Polismin has big feet; they also has caps, an coats with black buttins, likewise trousirs. Sum polismin is sargints, an wers stripes, and other polismin is notin only polismin. Polismin is niver to be seen whin there is eny divarshen, sich as fitin, ett setra, goin on. But whin there is notin at all goin on, only me an dother young chaps plain lep-frog, thin polismin cums buzzin round us like bees round a cask. Polismin has sum times a soort iv a thing called a clue—but the divil a know I know what it is, at all, at all. Me Uncle Tom sez it's all a cod! He sez, whin polismin wants to see there names in newspapers they tells thim min calld reportirs that they hav a clue, but the divil resave the clue they hav about thim at all. Me Uncle Tom hates polismin like anything, an they are all as fond iv him as the divil is iv holy water. You see, they wanst took me Uncle Tom for fitin Peet Linch, an—all bekaze Peet called him a 'tailer's gudgon.' It took 9 polismin to take me Uncle Tom to the station, an whin they got him there the half iv thim wor 'horse de combat' the papers sed. You see, me Uncle Tom is what they call 'kitogue'—which manes that he fites wid his left fist. So, iv coorse, whin you think he is goin to land you wid his right, begorra, you die wid surprise whin he ups wid his left an tumbils you! Me Uncle Tim is a great politishion, havin been in prison 14 times. He sez wan more indurance vile will make him a Martha— what iver the mischif that is. Me Uncle Tom is what they call excintrick in his timper whin he has a glass or 2. That's why polismin don't like him. But, shur, wate till I tell you: A polisman wanst cum coortin me cosin Kate. He was a tall polisman wid side whiskers, an as tin as a match. It wood take 2 min like him to make a shado. Well, me dear, he coorted me cosin Kate for 6 monts, an me Uncle Tom didn't know a haport about the goins on. But wan fine day he ketches thim out wakin together, an him wid his arm round her waste, iv you plaze! Me Uncle Tom immadiatly ups wid his fut an gives the polisman a riser which gev him a full vue iv the surrondin cenery. An whin he cum down agin, he cum down sittin, and thin ups and tells me Uncle Tom that he wood prosicut him for a salt an battry. You may be sure this riz me Uncle Tom! 'What!' siz he. '*You!*' siz he. '*You* prosicut *me!*' siz he. 'You misrable ixcuse for a man!' siz he. 'Look here,' siz he, 'do you kno what it is?' siz he— 'if you don't git up out iv that,' siz he, 'an go on out iv this,' siz he, 'be japers, I'll kick the suspinders off you!' An so begorra, wid that, the polisman riz up an wint. No more at prisint from

"Patsey O'Brien."

As I finish the recitation of Master O'Brien's essay, I catch the sound of a low, musical laugh, and turning round, see that a lady is seated in the kitchen in conversation with Mrs. McBride. Heavens, what a pair of dark-grey eyes! What a wealth of wavy brown hair!

I keep Patsey in chat, instead of proceeding on my way. I ask him all sorts of questions, though his answers fall on deaf ears. At length *she* comes out.

" Well, Mrs. McBride," she says, " tell Bartle that I am quite in love with the baby."

" That I will, miss ! " answers the proud mother.

" And that I will come and see him again soon."

" Thank you kindly, miss."

" And now good-bye for the present."

" Good-bye, miss, until we see you agin."

And the beautiful stranger turns and departs.

" Who is that nice-looking lady, Mrs. McBride ? " I ask.

"Begorra, shure, that's me landlord," she answers.

"Your *landlord?*"

"Yis, sur, that's Miss Ethel Foyle, the owner iv Grange Foyle."

"Oh, indeed," I exclaim. "Why, I thought Miss Foyle was abroad."

"So she was, sur; but she cum back home a day ago wid her aunt, Miss Martha. An' shure she wasn't long in cummin to see me an' the babby! But she's a darlint!"

"She is certainly very pretty," I say.

"That she is, sur! An' shure she was only eighteen last month. An' didn't she laugh whin she heerd you readin' out what little Patsey writ! An' thin she wanted to know all about you."

"Did she really?"

"Yis, sur; so av coorse I towld her you war here for the fishin'."

Here Master McBride is heard waking the echoes, and his mother hastens to him, while I go round to my den *viâ* the front door.

\* \* \* \* \*

After luncheon I begin to feel in the blues, so decide on a walk to O'Hara Castle. Ethel Foyle! Ethel Foyle! The name keeps ringing in my ears as I walk along the quiet road. Those dark-grey eyes peep out at me from every bush and brier along the way. Ethel Foyle! Ethel Foyle! I fear me, I have met my fate at last!

When I reach Ballyboyle it is to find it very much alive. Dragoons are wandering all over the place; officers' servants are busy exercising horses; officers' wives and children are popping in and out of shops; soldiers' wives and children are carrying baskets, and bags laden with provisions, towards the barracks. Cars, wagonettes, and phaetons rattle along the roadway. A travelling circus has pitched its tent in the old market-place, and "The only Original Spotted Boy" is on view (admission one penny) round by the post-office. Ballyboyle is certainly wide awake! Even the dogs have no time for scratching; and I saw just now a gossoon with a boot on. It was only a single boot—what there was of it—and had evidently not been made to measure; but still it was a boot, or the remains of one.

When I come to the office of the *Ballyboyle Examiner* I find Mr. O'Hara busy writing a leader on the "Ballyboyle Renaissance."

"Ah, is it there you are!" he cries, jumping up and grasping my hand. "I'm as glad as a shilling you've come! I've got an order for the circus to-night—an order for two. We'll go there after dinner. A real live circus, with two clowns, and a performing pig! Think of that, Master Brook!"

"Thanks to the *Examiner*," I say.

"You're right, sur—I own the soft impeachment. Come along—we'll take Duffy's on the way. I want to order some whisky."

I dine with the great Editor, get a front seat with him at the circus, and altogether have a pleasant time of it.

When I reach home the following telegram from Langton awaits me—

"*Nothing serious with Madge. Will be with you in a day or so.*"

That's all right. And now to bed.

## CHAPTER XV.

#### CAPTAIN TEMPEST.

THE Mullinbeg Races begin to-morrow. Madge, fit and well, has arrived, and is located in the Mill stables. Tempest's crack, the Shah, is stabled in Ballyboyle, and the Captain himself is staying here in the Mill-house, having arrived last Monday. A dark, handsome, Spanish-looking man is the Captain, with military moustache and piercing eyes. That moustache seems to partly conceal an almost perpetual grin. The instant he entered the sitting-room on the night of his arrival, this grin appeared to become emphasized for an instant, as he took in the whole contents of the apartment in a glance. When his eyes rested on me they actually seemed to twinkle with an amused sparkle. After we had been introduced by Langton, he asked—

"Have you been here long, Mr. Dolan?"

"Some weeks," I answered.

"Ah, I suppose you have taken quite a fancy to this old mill."

"Yes," I said, "I am rather fond of it."

Again he surveyed the room with those piercing eyes of his. Its plain furniture and simple ornaments seemed to afford him such ill-concealed amusement that I asked—

"But how comes it that you have chosen this shabby old place?"

"Because it was my humour," he replied.

"I thought it was for the sake of the fishing," said Langton abruptly.

"Well, yes, that possibly had something to do with it." Then turning to me he continued—"I presume you are a regular Walton?"

"No, not altogether," I declared; "but I am very fond of trout-fishing."

"By the way, Tempest, I was not aware that you were given to angling," Langton remarked. "I thought you devoted your entire talents to racing."

"My dear boy, you have no right to think anything whatever on the matter," answered the Captain, in a tone which made the blood flush in Langton's face. He was about to reply, but checked himself.

Then the Captain, turning to me again, continued—

"I suppose the attendance here is of a rough-and-ready order? Servants not exactly those we meet with in London?"

"Oh, the attendance is very fair," I answered. "Mrs. McBride attends to us herself."

"Ah, I see—but still, I think a nice blue-eyed, golden-haired English girl as waitress would be much better—eh?"

And with another emphasized grin the Captain strolled out to the front and lit a cigar.

"Well, Arthur, what do you think of him?" asked Langton.

"Well, it is hardly time enough to pass judgment yet," I answered. "I can't exactly make him out. He may be all right, but he has a very unprepossessing manner."

"I *don't* like the beggar!" exclaimed my friend. "I don't know why, but I don't."

"Oh, he may be all right when you know him."

"Yes, but you've got to know him *just*. I hope he won't suspect my feelings towards him."

"Why?" I asked.

"Because I believe he would enjoy the business of making himself ten times as disagreeable. That's the sort of man he is."

"Well, if that is your opinion, you should do all in your power to make him think you rather liked him."

"Just so, Arthur—but I'm a bad actor."

Presently we went out and joined the Captain, who was sitting beside the window smoking.

"What about your horse, Tempest?" began Langton, lighting his pipe. "Is he going to win?"

"Can't say," he answered—"is yours?"

"Can't say; but she will have a good

try. Your horse ought to win the hurdle-race, though; he seems a ripper."

"Well, we shall see what we shall see," is all the answer Tempest vouchsafed, and then relapsed into silence.

Presently he rose, jerked his cigar away, and with a "Good-night, you fellows," went off to his room.

"I wonder if he has backed his horse?" I asked.

"Goodness knows, Arthur. I have heard a whisper that the Shah was half-owned by Sandhiem."

"What! Sandhiem the bookmaker?"

"The same; but then such yarns are told about every other horse. At the same time it's remotely probable that the Shah is not all Tempest's property."

"After all, what does it matter to us?" I said, laughing.

"Nothing, absolutely nothing, Arthur;

but the beggar is so deep—that is, in *my* opinion—that I'd just like to know all about him."

"Well, you'll know all about his horse this time next Thursday, Jack."

"Yes, and all about my own too!"

And by and by we sought our pillows —Jack to dream of Madge winning in a hack canter, and I to dream of a pair of dark eyes.

\* \* \* \* \*

As I have said, the races begin to-morrow, and Langton is in a fever over Madge's final grooming. Tempest, on the contrary, takes things easy. Since he came he has only visited his horse's stable once, and has spent most of his time in strolling about the mill. Sometimes he has paused in his walk to admire the baby, much to Mrs. McBride's delight. He informed her yesterday that it was the finest child for its age he had ever seen. Indeed, he seems to have taken quite a fancy to Master McBride, as that young gentleman reposes in his nurse's arms. Liz seems to be as proud of the baby as Mrs. McBride herself, if smiles and blushes go for anything.

By the way, I quite forgot to mention that the Captain brought, along with the rest of his luggage, a guitar; and yesterday evening he carried it out to the seat outside the window, and told us he would sing a song, just to please the baby. So telling Liz to sit down beside him with Master McBride in her arms, he sang the following song in a rich, mellow baritone voice. And as the music floated through the evening air, it seemed by some mysterious power to draw the whole household, Mrs. McBride, Bartle, Langton, and myself, round him. He called the song—

## ROSY JUNE.

It is the merry month of June,
   When roses smell the sweetest;
When brightly burnished sails the moon,
   And nights are of the fleetest.

And oh, but 'tis a sunny time—
   The dearest time for wooing,
For whispering a loving rhyme,
   For billing and for cooing.

Come, wrecker of my peace of mind !
   We'll take a walk together.
In honour of the month I'll bind
   Thy wavy hair with heather.

I'll show thee the enchanted dell,
   Within whose magic portals
White fairy-bells grow, hidden well
   From thieving hands of mortals.

To yonder isle I'll row you o'er;
   We'll make a fan of rushes;
And when I tell my love once more,
   'Twill do to hide your blushes.

## CHAPTER XVI.

### AT THE RACES.

FIRST day of the Mullinbeg races! Work suspended everywhere; the mill silent, and its wheel asleep. Everybody in his, or her, Sunday clothes, making for the " coorse." Tempest started early, while Langton and I do not reach the scene until about twenty minutes before the first race. The grand stand is brave with all the " quality " in the county—pretty women in charming costumes, and ruddy-faced men in the " latest cuts." The course is crowded with countrymen, with their wives and sweethearts, all engaged in the congenial task of enjoying themselves by dancing, drinking, and courting. Surveying the scene from the grand stand enclosure, I suddenly catch sight of a man standing by the ticket gate. With hands in pockets he gazes vacantly about him, as if quite uninterested in anything. He wears an old straw hat, a shabby frieze coat, corduroy trousers, and well-greased brogues, while round his neck is a faded green silk handkerchief. There are dozens of men almost his exact counterpart to be seen on the course, but I could pick him out from among a thousand of them. The instant I see him I proceed to walk hastily towards him.

"Where are you going?" calls Langton.

"I'll be back presently," I call back.

"You'll be late for the race!"

I make no reply, for at this moment the man I am making for descries me, and moving quickly away, is soon lost among the crowd on the course. No matter, I am determined on running him down. Leaving the enclosure, I mingle with the crowd, and peep into every tent, overlook every dancing-party, pay a penny and become one of the audience at the Fat Lady's reception, but all to no purpose; my man is still missing. I am returning, and have just reached the enclosure gate, when I see him. He is in the act of dodging round to the back of the stands— a deserted field with a few stumps of trees standing here and there. Now I've got him! Quickly I make my way round after him, and presently come upon him quietly smoking, as he reclines on the grass behind one of the stumps. He sees me ere I reach him, but knows it is too late to escape.

"Now then, Watts, what have you done with Alice?"

"Ah, Mr. Dolan, is that you?" he

exclaims, as if seeing me for the first time. "And how are you?"

"I'm all right; but I want to know about this Alice mystery. You are a detective; I know all about you."

"Yes, I am a detective," he answers, taking his pipe from his lips, and placing it on the grass beside him. "I am a detective, Mr. Dolan."

"Well, then, tell me about this Alice business—why was she arrested?"

"Sit down here beside me, Mr. Dolan," he says, "and I'll tell you all I am allowed to tell."

I take my place beside him on the grass, and as I do, the shouting and cheering on the course tells me that the first race is over.

"Now, go ahead," I say. "You came down to the mill in search of the girl?"

"By your leave, sur, I did nothing of

the kind," he declares, smiling. "There you are wrong. I went to the mill, as I told you, on leave. But on the night of me arrival I recognized her—as we had her photograph in the head office in Dublin. Next morning I drove into Ballyboyle in time to dispatch a letter by the first train asking for a warrant."

"A warrant!"

"Yes, sur—for her detention."

"What is her real name?"

"She was known as Alice Long," replies Mr. Watts, after a pause.

"Well, about the warrant?"

"Don't you remember a large blue envelope coming, with five shillings to pay?"

"Yes, very well."

"Well, sur, that was the warrant. The instant I got it I left you alone, if you remember. I went and saw Alice and told her who I was, showing her the warrant.

I remained in the sitting-room all that night, fearing she might attempt to come down and escape."

"Yes, I remember all that, Watts. But what crime did the girl commit? that's what I want to know."

"No crime at all, sur," answered Mr. Watts; "no crime at all. Make your mind easy on *that* point."

"No crime of any sort?"

"None, sur."

"Then why, in the name of Heaven, procure a warrant against her?" I ask in surprise.

"That I cannot tell you, sur." And Mr. Watts proceeds to light his pipe.

"Why can't you tell me?"

"Because she herself made me solemnly promise to say nothing on the matter to any one. And now, Mr. Dolan, you know all I've got to tell you."

"What can this mystery be?" I say, rising.

"That's none of *my* affairs, sur," answers Mr. Watts, following suit. "I did me duty. I knew you would be questioning me, and that was me reason for trying to keep out of your way."

"And where is she now?"

"In England, sur. And now I must get back to the course; I am on duty here to-day."

"Indeed!"

"Yes. Some of us chaps are down from Dublin, just to keep our eyes open for sharps. Do you bet at all, Mr. Dolan?"

"Now and again, if I get anything really straight."

"Well, look here, sur, I'll tell you what's going to win the big race, and it will be sure to start at good odds—the Shah."

"Oh, you think the Shah will win?"

"I *know* he will, Mr. Dolan, bar accidents. Us chaps gets things straight sometimes, and I happen to know that Captain Tempest has backed his horse for a heap of money."

"But won't that make the animal start at short odds?"

"No, sur; they are going to serve up two hot favourites. Wait, and you'll see."

"By the way, Captain Tempest is staying with us at the Mill-house."

"What!" exclaims Watts in a tone of surprise. Then after walking a few steps he adds, half to himself, "Just like him—just like him!"

"Do you know him, Watts?"

Watts does not reply for a moment. Then he asks—

"Is he a friend of yours, Mr. Dolan?"

"Well, no. I never met him until he came to the mill."

"Well then, sur, I'll give you a piece of advice—trust Captain Tempest as little as you possibly can. Now I must leave you."

Bidding him good-bye, I make my way round to the stand. Looking about for Langton, I suddenly light on him as he is holding animated converse with a very handsome woman—dark, dressed in crimson, and full of dimples. But it is her companion my eyes rest on, for her companion is Ethel Foyle. There she stands, dressed in dazzling white, her big dark eyes looking brighter than ever, and a little rosy hue in her cheeks. Now she turns to speak with an elderly lady who stands a little behind her. That elderly lady is her aunt, and the dark, dimply form in crimson is Mrs. Desmond. Now for an introduction to my Fate! I am making my way towards them, when I meet Mr. O'Hara.

"Oh, there you are!" he cries. "I've

been looking for you everywhere. Your friend's horse won't win this race after all."

"Oh, is Madge in the next race?" I ask.

"Why, of course she is!" he answers. "Didn't you know that? Why, they are on their way to the post now. But the Craneen will win."

"Sure?"

"Certain, Mr. Dolan—have just got it straight. I was full sure Madge would walk away with it; but the Craneen has got back all her two-year-old form, and will win, hands down. Now I must to my post—I'm on the Press stand." And off he goes.

When I reach Langton and the ladies, the former exclaims—

"Oh, here you are! Why, where on earth have you been—eh?" And then he introduces me to Dimples, Miss Martha, and —my Fate.

"I have been admiring my namesake, Madge," Mrs. Dimples — no, Desmond — tells me; "and I hope she is going to win."

"I'm afraid not," I answer. "The Craneen will about win, I am informed."

"Oh, don't say that!" she exclaims; "I shall be ever so much disappointed if Madge does not win by at least twenty lengths."

"I'm afraid my friend is right," Langton says, laughing. "He is the luckiest tipster extant; he would make his fortune as a sporting prophet. But let us return to the stand, Mrs. Desmond, the race will start immediately."

On to the stand we go—I between Miss Martha and my Fate. What a row the bookmakers are causing with their raucous shouting!

"Four-to-one on the fee-oold! Four-to-one on the fee-oold! Four-to-one against the Craneen! Four-to-one the Craneen does not win! Five-to-one against Madge!" etc., etc.

Miss Foyle is asking me to explain to her why they should persist in calling the field, the "fee-oold," when a mighty shout, "They're off!" tells us that the race has started.

Every glass is directed away towards the right, where the seven runners are seen coming along in a cluster.

"Oh, where is Madge?" ask Mrs. Desmond.

"Close *behind* the others," I tell her.

"Yes," adds Langton, "but she seems to be gaining!"

"Ah, the Craneen is drawing out," I say, keeping my glass upon the favourite.

"Where is Madge now?" Miss Foyle inquires.

"Fourth."

"But, by Jove, she is beginning to wake up!" cries Langton. "She won't be far away at the finish!"

He is right. In another couple of minutes, amidst a storm of cheers, the Craneen comes in winner, with Madge a good second.

"There!" cries Mrs. Desmond, her brown eyes sparkling with pleasure. "She is actually second!"

"Which is the next best thing to being first," declares her cousin.

"Now let us go and have a look at the winner," says Langton, offering his arm to Mrs. Desmond.

"Oh, bother the winner!" she exclaims; "I only want to see Madge."

Down we go from the stand and proceed towards the paddock, I personally conducting Miss Foyle and her aunt—the latter assuring me *en route* that she had dreamt last night of a dark-brown horse winning a race.

"That was a wonderful dream!" I declare. "The Craneen *is* a dark-brown horse."

"Yes, it is really very wonderful," the dear old lady continues, while Miss Foyle smiles a humorous little smile; "all my dreams seem to come true, though my nieces laugh when I say so."

After we have inspected the winner, as in duty bound, and have had a look at Madge, we return to the stand, and await the issue of the big race. But I take no particular interest in its approach; I take no interest in anything around me. My whole thoughts are centred in the "woman in white" who is by my side. How I wish the races were over, and that she and I were walking down some silent lane! or seated together in some cosy nook overhung with dark-green boughs, and with a brook singing away at our feet.

But one cannot help hearing those awful bookmakers. Casting a glance of scorn, indignation, and contempt towards them, I see that amongst their number is Sandhiem. Yes, hook-nosed *Sheeny Sandhiem*, as the Cockney punters call him. There he stands in close conversation with Tempest. Ho! ho! I wonder how many shares has he in " Shah stock "!

## CHAPTER XVII.

### I SCORE AGAINST THE CAPTAIN.

I AM in nice, quiet conversation with Miss Foyle, when, happening to look round, I find Tempest standing beside me. At the same moment Mrs. Desmond notices him.

"Ah, Captain Tempest," she says, "who would have thought of meeting you here?"

"Well, you see, Mrs. Desmond, I have a horse running here," he answers, as he shakes hands with her, much to Langton's evident surprise. "I am running the Shah."

"Oh, yes; I see now," continues Mrs. Desmond, looking over the entries on the card. "Are you going to win?"

"No," he answers; "I think Kilkee will win."

"Who is that gentleman?" Miss Foyle asks me aside.

"Don't you know him?" I answer. "He is Captain Tempest, the racing man."

"Why should you think I know him?" she wants to know.

"Well, as your cousin knows him, of course I thought you would have known him also."

"You forget, that while my cousin has been in London I have been abroad," she says.

"Do you intend remaining at home now for good?"

"Perhaps," she answers, after a little pause.

Meantime Tempest has turned towards us, and I can see his eyes light up with admiration as he looks at Miss Foyle. How he must envy me! That's a comforting thought! Presently he asks me, with the old momentary grin—

"What have you backed for this race, Mr. Dolan?"

"Nothing."

"Ah, that's very foolish," he observes, shaking his head—"very foolish indeed. Now, will you take my advice?"

"What is it?"

"Go at once and back Kilkee; I have done so."

"What! and your own horse running?"

"Yes, and my own horse running, as you truly remark. But my own horse has no chance; I was deceived by others, or I would never have brought him over. However, as he is here, I am letting him run—just for exercise, don't you know. Kilkee is the winner."

"Then you really think it good?" I say.

"Why, have I not said so?" he answers. "Go and put a couple of hundred on."

"Yes, my dear fellow, that's all very well; but I didn't come prepared to bet in hundreds, and I never back on the nod."

"My dear fellow," he exclaims, "don't allow that to detain you for a moment. I'll oblige you with two hundred. Why didn't you ask me?"

"You're very kind," I answer, while I am conscious that Miss Foyle looks at me in surprise.

Out comes Tempest's fat purse, and from it he takes four fifty-pound notes, which he hands to me with that *devil gleam*, as Langton called it, in his eye.

"Thanks. Kilkee, you say?"

"Yes; hurry and get on, or you'll be late."

"What bookmaker will I select? Can you recommend one?"

"Oh, yes," and his eyes actually twinkle. "Sandhiem is your man. There he is—the man with the white hat."

"All right," I say; and then turning to Miss Foyle I continue, "Pray excuse my leaving you for a moment—I am going to back a horse."

She merely nods her head, without answering (which I would think a little bit rude in any other woman), and down I go to the ring. Sandhiem is waiting for me, though he does not appear to notice me until I accost him.

"Well, Sandhiem, what price the favourite?"

"Three-to-one, sir; four-to-one Mullabie. My book is heavy against both."

"Three-to-one, Kilkee, did you say?"

"Yes, sir; and I tell you straight, I don't care to lay any more against her. But, as you are——"

"Tell me—what price the Shah? I know the owner, and would like to have a bit on, though he tells me it has no chance."

Here one of the bookmakers cries, "Ten-to-one the Shah."

"You hear that, sir?" says Sandhiem, smiling.

"Yes, ten-to-one. Well, I'll take three pounds to one about Kilkee," and opening my purse, I hand him a sovereign.

"Right, sir," and Sandhiem books the bet to me.

"Now I think I'll have a bit on the Shah, just for the owner's sake."

"Very good, sir;" and Sandhiem puts on a very broad grin for my benefit. "You know the price—tens?"

"Yes, there you are;" and I hand him the two hundred pounds. "I'll take two thousand to two hundred the Shah."

The smile vanishes, and Sandhiem actually starts. Then he gives me a quick, keen glance, and says—

"You seem to fancy the horse?"

"Book my bet, please."

"Yes, sir;" and down goes the bet into Sandhiem's book.

When I return to the stand, it is to find Tempest beside Miss Foyle, and, moreover, conversing with her. In fact, so interested do they appear in their conversation, that they take no notice of my presence. With a curious pang of—what? jealousy and hatred, I suppose—I turn and begin talking gaily with Miss Martha. Suddenly Tempest condescends to notice me.

"Ah, there you are!" he exclaims, with that infernal gleam of triumph in his eyes. "Well, did you back Kilkee?"

"Yes, at three to one."

"They're off!" is roared forth at this

moment, and we all raise our glasses, and watch the race. I need not describe it in full. Mullabie falls at the third hurdle, leaving eleven still on their legs. Kilkee gives in ere two miles are over.

"Ah, your money is lost—I'm so sorry," cries Tempest, turning to me. "Kilkee will be absolutely last."

I do not answer. By this time they have galloped past us on the first round. Gradually the Shah improves his pace, and when they are coming home he is leading by three lengths, and eventually wins easily.

"Just fancy, my horse winning—and winning in a canter, Miss Foyle!" says the Captain.

"I am very glad of your good fortune," she answers.

"Indeed I am glad *some* horse has won," remarks Miss Martha. "I knew it would."

"My dear Dolan, I'm so sorry you lost that two hundred on Kilkee," Tempest says, turning to me—"*so* sorry."

"Oh, I only lost a sovereign on Kilkee," I say quietly.

"Only a sovereign!" he exclaims. "And what did you do with the rest?"

"The rest? Oh, you mean the two hundred I had from you?"

"Yes—what did you do with it?"

"Put it all on the Shah, at ten-to-one."

Ha, ha! I've knocked that devil out of your eye for once, my gallant Captain.

By this time all are on their way to the paddock, Tempest escorting Miss Foyle. But instead of following, I make haste to Sandhiem for my winnings. He pays me per cheque, though I insist on having my stakes back in notes.

Presently I go to Tempest, and hand him the notes with many thanks.

"How did you come to fancy my horse?" he asks.

"Because I knew it was going to win," I answer, and then join Langton and Mrs. Desmond.

When I tell the former of my luck he beams with delight.

"Dolan's luck again," he exclaims. "How I should have liked to watch Tempest's face!"

"Yes, it was a study."

We three—Langton, Tempest, and myself—go back to Grange Foyle to dinner.

## CHAPTER XVIII.

### GRANGE FOYLE.

Langton, Tempest, and myself left for the mill before the last race, which gave us ample time to dress and start for Grange Foyle by half-past seven. I, as usual, was ready first, and dropped into Langton's room to hurry him.

"How is it you never told me you knew Mrs. Desmond?" I asked him.

"I don't know," he answered.

"You don't know! Are you sure of that, Jack?"

"Well, the fact is, Arthur, I thought you might begin your confounded chaff, and perhaps fancy that she was the cause of my coming over to Ireland, don't you know."

"I don't fancy it at all—I *know* it."

"Oh, indeed! Well, then, perhaps you will keep the knowledge to yourself."

"Certainly, my dear Jack, I'll keep as dark as the lady's eyes. But only to think of a woman converting you!"

"What do you mean by converting me?" he asked sharply.

"Why, I mean that you, who were the most anti——"

"There! there! if you love me, Arthur, cut it!"

"Well, then, I won't tease you further," I said. "And all I hope is, that the lady may capture you—or you the lady. It's all the same."

"Amen!" exclaimed Langton.

After lighting a cigarette, and puffing at it vigorously for a minute, I asked—

"How did Mrs. Desmond come to know Tempest?"

"Met him in London," Langton answered. " By the way, he seemed to have completely cut you out to-day."

" In what way, pray ? "

"Why, he made all the running with Miss Foyle."

"Oh, I didn't mind that," I declared. "I suppose he is the sort of man young ladies like."

Langton did not answer, and presently I left him, and going down to the hall, found Tempest talking to the baby, who reclined in the arms of Liz.

" Oh, there you are at last ! " he exclaimed. " What a time you mashers take to dress ! Where is Langton ? "

"Here I am," answered Jack, coming down the stairs. " We have plenty of time."

\* \* \* \* \*

The car that has taken us from the mill

is now rolling along the Grange Foyle avenue, which is bordered on either side by a band of flowers backed by shrubs. The combined odour of both is very grateful, and makes Langton exclaim—

"Bless my soul! And this is an Irish avenue!"

"Yes," answers Tempest. "I presume you are wondering where the pigs are."

Langton doesn't answer him, and presently we reach the house—a grey granite building, almost completely mantled in light-green ivy. A flight of Kilkenny marble steps leads to the door, from whence we can survey the beautiful park, studded with its ringed plantations of pine and fir, round which the rabbits love to play.

\*　　\*　　\*　　\*　　\*

We are seated at dinner in a long, oak-panelled room, from whose ceiling hang two silver candelabra, bearing wax-lights all aglow. Over the black marble chimney-piece stands a full-length portrait of the first Lord Crogan—a florid-looking gentleman in a white wig and plum-coloured velvet coat, white satin knee-breeches, white silk stockings, and very shiny shoes with high heels and diamond buckles. His lordship also wears a sword with blue enamelled handle, upon which his crest is blazoned in small diamonds. Other paintings of former hosts and hostesses of Grange Foyle are ranged round the room. Some of the ladies must have been beauties.

But to return from the dead and gone to the quick and present—how handsome Mrs. Desmond looks in her light-grey dinner dress, and how happy! But is not Langton seated on her left?—Happy beggar! Ethel, looking lovelier than ever, is in pink, and also in deep thought. Perhaps it is Tempest's words to her which make her look so thoughtful. He has had the proud privilege of taking her in to dinner. She has bestowed just two passing glances in my direction since we sat down. And we were getting on so well before Tempest intervened! Well, if the lady prefers the gallant captain to all other champions in Christendom, who shall say her nay? Not I for one.

How I wish this confounded dinner over! The chatter, chatter, chatter of those around grates terribly on my ears. There is one old lady in shot-silk, and gifted with a high-pitched Cork brogue, who is quite enough to drive a man to desperation. Belfast! Mayo! Galway! forgive me, ye three! In days gone by I declared the brogue of your citizens to be the most truly awful in Ireland. I was wrong—I uttered a base calumny! Cork, "Rebel Cork" —it rebelled against its chosen chief—beats ye all into matchwood as a rouser of all that is fierce and murderous in man.

That old red-faced, choleric-looking man with the glazed head also annoys me. He is Sir James O'Tyrrell—the gentleman who so miraculously escaped the slugs of the twilight assassin. He is narrating the occurrence to his neighbour on the right —an uncertain aged lady with a pronounced Roman nose and a garnet necklace.

"Just imagine for one moment, Miss Muldoon," he is saying, "just imagine a person so popular—I may be allowed to say, so universally popular—as I am, being fired at! Did you ever hear of such a thing?"

Miss Muldoon admits that she never did, and adds—

"The ruffians will never be caught, of course—they never are."

"Not they, my dear Miss Muldoon," continues Sir James. "Not they, indeed! The country is in a deplorable state—a deplorable state!"

Seated beside me is Miss Fanny Dunne of Dunkiel, who, I believe, is one of the county belles. She has large, languishing hazel eyes, raven hair, and an olive complexion. She is author, or authoress, of two sporting novels, and composer—or composeress (?) — of a rattle-can galop, which was rather popular with the Kingstown, Bray, and Dalkey bands last season. But she is not a bit like a genius, thank goodness, and has a splendid appetite. She has been grumbling a bit at not being able to visit London this season, but consoles herself with the thought that, after all, the country is the best of all possible places. In this I quite agree with her.

"And do *you* really prefer the country to town?" she asks.

"Yes, in the summer and autumn," I answer. "Give me the south of Europe in the winter."

"And London in spring, I suppose?"

"There is no spring in London," I tell her. "What is spring elsewhere is only a severe relapse of winter in England."

"What is your idea of an ideal life of happiness?" she queries. "What sort of a home would you select?"

"A roomy cottage, in the centre of about two hundred acres of land, containing a little wood and water, and with a good fruit, flower, and kitchen-garden."

"Rather modest in your wish," she says, smiling and thinking of old Dunkiel with its five thousand acres, its gardens, conservatories, orchards, and home park.

"Yes," I continue. "I *am* modest in my aspirations. I sold my property—house, land, and all that—simply because I was too modest to get into debt in order to uphold the traditional position of my family."

It is always well to let women know who you are—if you happen to be anybody.

"What a pity!" Miss Dunne remarks; but whether her sorrow is for the loss of my home, or for my foolishness in not getting into debt, I cannot tell.

"But, to continue, Miss Dunne—I think two hundred acres of land with wood and water, and a well-built dwelling-house, ought to content any man."

"Why do you insist on the wood and water?" she wants to know.

"Because they would both lure the birds; the trees would shelter the summer birds, and the pond would give sanctuary to our winter visitors—coot, widgeon, and duck, for instance. Of course I would have a few sheep, a cow or two, and horses."

"Oh, yes—horses by all means!" she exclaims. "Good horses!"

"Yes, not to mention dogs," I add. "Good dogs!"

Miss Dunne's bilious-eyed, sallow-faced,

Anglo-Indian mamma, who sits opposite us, has been regarding me critically for the last few minutes through her gold-rimmed glasses. I detest the whole tribe of calculating mothers.

"Why is that old lady watching me so intently?" I ask Miss Dunne. "Do you know who she is?"

"Who?" queries Miss Dunne, looking at every old lady but the right one.

"Who?—why, that old lady seated opposite."

"Oh, that's only mamma," she explains.

And then we lapse into silence.

\* \* \* \* \*

Ten o'clock; moon shining bright outside; drawing-room ornamented with fair women and brave men; Miss Dunne at piano, singing something about yesterday and sorrow, and oh give me back to-morrow—at least, that is all I can make out of it.

Perhaps I am not paying proper attention. Perhaps my thoughts are wandering with my glances to where Ethel Foyle and that fiend Tempest are seated. Bah! this won't do; I'll pack up and leave the mill for London. Yet *she* does not appear to be very, *very* happy to-night, and I notice that Tempest is doing most of the talking. There! that's the second time she has glanced towards me——

Enter quietly through door leading from conservatory Mrs. Desmond looking extremely demure. She takes a seat beside Miss Dunne's mamma, who begins a narrative about her lost liver. Elapse of one minute. Enter through door leading from conservatory John Langton, who drops into nearest chair, and appears speechless with rapture at Miss Dunne's warbling. Tableau.

## CHAPTER XIX.

### LANGTON IS LANDED.

MIDNIGHT finds the car containing Langton and myself on its homeward journey from Grange Foyle. Tempest elected to drive back with one Captain Lynch, who had a fast trotter, and was bound to pass the mill. How glad I was when I saw them depart! The idea of travelling on the same car with that hated, grinning, fiend was anything but pleasant to me.

I sit on one side of the car, Langton on the other, while the driver, who I am happy to say is deaf as a post, occupies the " dickey." I smoke in silence. Langton is also silent, so far as talk is concerned, but he seems to have suddenly contracted a cough. This cough irritates me beyond endurance.

"Langton, where did you catch that new cough?" I inquire at length.

"Who—I?"

"Yes, you."

He does not answer, but the cough ceases, and gradually I begin to forget all about him, the cough, and everything, as my thoughts turn back towards Grange Foyle, and the fair jewel it enshrines.

"I say, Arthur—it's all right."

His words startle me, as from a dream.

"What's all right?" I listlessly inquire.

"Why, *I* am."

"That's all right," I say, yawning; the clear air is making me sleepy.

"I was awfully nervous—egad I was!" he continues.

"Is that so?"

"Yes, wouldn't *you* have been?"

"What the devil *are* you talking about?" I exclaim, rousing myself at last.

"What am I talking about?" he echoes. "Why, what a stupid chap you are! I am talking about Madge, of course."

"Well, what about Madge?" I ask. "She was a good second—what are you nervous about?"

Here he breaks into a laugh—a laugh so loud and long that our driver actually fancies he hears something, and looks round inquiringly.

"Arthur! Arthur! you're a blockhead!" comes when the laugh is at last finished.

"Probably I am, but hang me if I can see what there is to laugh about!"

"Why, man alive, I was not alluding to Madge the horse!"

"No?"

"No—I was speaking of Madge Desmond—my Madge!"

"Oh, now I am enlightened!" I exclaim. "You have proposed to Mrs. Desmond?"

"Yes, and she has accepted me;" and he slaps me on the back. One would think that she had accepted *me!*

"I'm delighted to hear it, Jack," I say, grasping his big, broad, honest English hand. "Delighted, my dear old chappie! When is the happy event coming off?"

"The wedding? Soon as possible."

"Where?"

"Here; then for a short trip to London and Paris, and then back here again. Madge has promised not to leave Ethel all alone in Grange Foyle for a year or so. But for that we would settle, after the honeymoon, in my old home. Now remember, Arthur, I claim you as best man."

"Ah, *you'll* be the best man on in that scene, Jack." I suppose it is something in the tone of my voice which keeps him so silent for a spell. But by and by, when we are nearing the mill, he suddenly asks—

"Arthur, why don't you marry and settle down?"

"I really don't know."

"You seemed to be getting on famously with that Miss Dunne during dinner. She is a fine woman."

"Do you think so?"

"Yes, don't you?"

"I have thought nothing at all about the matter," I reply; and then he leaves me alone.

When we get to the gate we leave the car and walk towards the house by the foot-path, which runs along by the garden hedge. Just at the end of it—ere you cross the race by the foot-bridge—we pass a man who stands close to the hedge.

"Who was that mysterious figure?" asks Langton, as we walk on. "He looked rather suspicious, standing there, and saying nothing."

"That was Shaun—the man I told you about."

"What man?"

"Why, Liz's fierce lover."

"Oh, I see; but what is he here at this time of night for?"

"On the off-chance of seeing her."

"What, at this time!" and Langton consults his watch by the moonlight. "Why, it's past one!"

We have approached within sight of the house as Langton speaks. Our coming disturbs two people who are talking inside the porch, and I catch the sound of a woman's feet hurrying away.

We find Tempest smoking at the door.

"Why, what a time you've taken!" he exclaims. "I have been home for nearly half-an-hour."

"And why the deuce didn't you go to bed?" I say.

"What!" he exclaims, with that maddening grin. "Sleep on such a heavenly night as this! This lovers' night, as poet fellows would call it! The idea of such a thing!"

"Are you a good hand at love-making?" I say, lighting a fresh cigar, and sitting down in the seat by the window.

"Sometimes," he answers—"when I am in the humour. I hope you enjoyed yourselves to-night— *I* have. Awfully nice women—awfully!"

"Are you going to run your horse to-morrow?" Langton wants to know.

"No, there are no more two thousands to be made," he replies. "What a lucky beggar you are, Dolan!"

"Yes, isn't he?" Langton cries. "Why, don't you know that 'Dolan's luck' is a common expression among our set in town?"

"Ah! how interesting!" remarks the Captain. "By the way, Langton, is your horse going to win to-morrow?"

"She is going to try?"

"Yes, but *is* she going to win—or, in other words, have you backed her?"

"I never back horses," answers Langton, stiffly.

"What, never? Well, I *am* surprised! After that I really must go to bed."

And so saying the Captain leaves us.

"How I should love to kick that man!" I say. "And it strikes me I will too, before I've done with him."

"Oh, leave him alone," advises Langton—"leave him alone. He will find his level at the finish."

"I devoutly hope so, Jack—I *hate* him!"

"Yes, I thought you would not fall in love with him."

At this moment I become conscious that

a face is peering towards us from the corner of the house. In a moment it is gone. It was the dark face of Shaun.

"Well, I'm off to bed," continues Langton, jumping up.

"Yes, to dream of *her*, you happy beggar!" I say, rising and following him into the house.

"Well, Arthur, why don't you follow my example?" he asks.

"What, and dream of her also?"

"No, confound you! Get some woman of your own to dream about. Good-night."

## CHAPTER XX.

### BY ETHEL'S SIDE.

I AM down first this morning, and while awaiting the others, go out and sit by the window. Liz is promenading up and down with the baby.

"Well, Liz, how is Shaun?"

"I don't know, sur," she answers, looking round quickly, as if she expected to see him somewhere about. By the way, I notice that the old blush and smile have vanished.

"Where were you this morning at one o'clock?" I ask, putting on a meaning smile.

"Why, in me bed, iv coorse, sur," she answers, and then turns and enters the house.

No, no, Liz, you were not in your bed!

Presently Tempest and Langton come down, and we proceed to breakfast.

"How is it you fellows can't get up early?" I say. "Here have I been down for the past half-hour."

"Well, have you not been amusing yourself the while?" says Tempest. "Mashing Liz, you sly dog!"

"I was not aware of the fact," I tell him.

"Oh, of course not," he continues, with that devil grin. "You forget that my window is over the door. I heard and saw you both this morning, you naughty, naughty man!"

Here Langton gives me a keen glance, but holds his peace, while I reply, reddening with annoyance—

"Don't talk such confounded nonsense, Tempest."

"There, there, don't blush," he exclaims.

"There is nothing terribly wrong in mashing a pretty nurse—they all do it."

"Ah, yes, you are quite right," I answer. "Some of them select the small hours of morning for it."

He leaves me alone after this, and we all three finish breakfasting in silence.

We arrive at the course in due time, and meet Mrs. Desmond, Ethel, and their aunt. Tempest immediately takes his place beside Ethel, and begins telling her of the delightful time he spent in Grange Foyle. I drop behind with Miss Martha, who starts a long story about her latest dream. I fear I do not pay much attention to her, though I manage to mutter an occasional "Indeed!" or "Dear me!"

The racing is more or less a repetition of yesterday's programme. There is no "big race," but to make up for the deficiency, we are treated to a "Members' Hunt

Hurdle-Race," a "Home County Farmers' Race," and a "Consolation Welter," during the progress of which one of the riders falls and breaks his leg — a very small consolation to *him*. Madge wins *her* race easily, to the unbounded delight of Mrs. Desmond.

We dine once more at Grange Foyle, and I have to endure the chatter of an emancipated female with a neck like a gander's, and possessing no apparent waist or breast. Why should it have fallen to my lot to bring such an object in to dinner, while Tempest walked off with Ethel Foyle? Is Dolan's luck deserting him?

"We women have remained slaves too long," the emancipated one is informing me.

"Indeed?"

"Yes; too long have we lain prone beneath the iron foot of our masculine oppressors. But the hour of our arising is close at hand! The spread of the higher culture, the writings of our advanced sisterhood, have lighted the refulgent illumination of dawning Emancipation."

"Ah, that's all right," I say in weariness.

"Yes," she continues, "we women are no longer of the weaker, but of the *stronger sex!*"

"Really?"

"Yes, we intend to enter Parliament."

"In a body?"

"No, not exactly in a body, but for each constituency."

"I presume you are an ardent Home Ruler?" I say.

"What!" she exclaims in horror, "*I* a Home Ruler! *I* who am a daughter of the most Conservative house in the county! Do you wish to offend me?"

"I beg your pardon, I'm sure," I hasten to say. "But the fact is, I have always been under the impression that all women were born to be Home Rulers. But then, of course, there is such a difference in women."

"I should think there was indeed!" she declares. "*I* was not born to be a Home Ruler."

"I don't suppose you were," I say; and at this moment, thank heaven, the ladies rise. Another five minutes and I would have grievously offended Miss—— Miss—— May I be shot if I can think of her name! However, I can always find it—it will never be changed.

By and by, when we join the ladies, I am before Tempest for once, and take my seat beside Ethel, while he turns, and selecting a chair beside Miss Martha, soon has that estimable old lady highly interested in his details of strange dreams and dreamers.

"I hope you enjoyed the racing to-day, Miss Foyle?" I venture to inquire.

"Yes, passably," she replies; "but I am not an enthusiastic lover of the sport, and as for betting, I abhor it!"

"There you are unlike most of your sex," I say. "As a rule, women are far greater gamblers, at heart, than men."

"Probably you are right," she admits; "but I detest both men and women who gamble."

"I certainly do not believe in betting myself," I tell her.

"You!" she answers with surprise. "Why, I thought you were a confirmed betting man."

I look at her in astonishment for a moment.

"Perhaps I am mistaken," she hastens to add.

"Completely!" I declare.

"I'm very sorry, Mr. Dolan—please forgive me!"

"Certainly—on one condition."

"What condition?" she wants to know.

"That you honestly tell me why you thought me a betting man."

She flushes a little, and then says—

"Well, you know you *left* me to go and put two hundred pounds on a horse."

"Oh, I see it all now," I exclaim. "No wonder you thought me a betting man."

"Yes," she continues; "and then I heard afterwards that you were called Lucky Dolan, on account of your betting transactions."

"Ah, pray, who told you that?"

"Well, I heard Mr. Langton say something about it to my cousin, and then Captain Tempest——"

"Pray say no more, Miss Foyle," I break in. "I presume whatever Captain Tempest told you about me must have been, to you, quite true."

"No, no, please, Mr. Dolan, don't think that," she pleads. "You see, you *left* me with the purpose of backing a horse with—with——"

"With the money I had borrowed from him."

She is silent, and I continue—

"Miss Foyle, I will on some future occasion tell you my reason—my hidden reason—for borrowing that money, and putting it on his horse."

"His horse won, did it not?" she asks.

"Yes; but if you remember, he declared that it had no chance whatever, and advised me to back Kilkee."

"Yes, I remember."

"Well, then, I knew he was wilfully deceiving me, and that he had backed his own horse for a large amount."

As I speak those big eyes grow bigger with mingled anger and astonishment.

"What a disgraceful act!" she cries. "What could be his motive in deceiving you?"

"It is the man's nature," I tell her. "He cannot help lying. Now let us talk about something more agreeable."

And what a long, long, lingering talk we have on music, poetry, the drama, art! My knowledge of the poets seems to perfectly astonish her.

"Why, Mr. Dolan," she says at length, "you ought to be a poet yourself."

"Perhaps I am—in the germ," I answer, laughing.

"But really you ought to write something," she continues. "I'm sure you could if you tried. Will you try?"

"Yes, since you ask me."

"I *do* ask you."

Here Mrs. Desmond and Langton put in an appearance. Where have they been all the time? I never saw such mysterious people. They seem to pass their time between appearing and disappearing.

"Your cousin looks particularly happy to-night, Miss Foyle."

"Yes," she answers, smiling. "I expect she looks as she feels."

"Of course my friend Langton has told me all about *his* happiness," I continue. "In fact, he has expressly engaged me as groomsman."

"Indeed!"

"Yes; I hope I shall fulfil the arduous duties to the utmost satisfaction."

"I hope so too," she says, with one of her musical laughs. "*I* also hope to please—I have been graciously presented with the post of chief bridesmaid. By the way, now is your chance to start as a poet, Mr. Dolan."

"In what way, pray?"

"Why, by writing an epithalamium."

"Ah! I fear wedding songs are out of date, Miss Foyle. In fact, it appears to me that everything poetic is out of date. We live in a prosaic age—an age of ruthless scientific analysis. Shakespeare and Kit Marlowe are replaced by Huxley and Tyndal. If a man gifted by the combined genius of Shakespeare and Milton were born to-morrow, he would live a life of starvation, and die in a hovel."

"Oh, do you think so?" she asks in wonder.

"I more than think it, Miss Foyle— I know it. A nation's life is the life of all things earthly — birth, growth, and decay. And a nation's progress and decline are as surely indicated by her literature, as the hour of twelve is marked by the shadow on a sundial. When Shakespeare and his mighty companion walked the streets of London, England was rising by leaps and bounds; and she sang aloud in her pride of health and strength—sang songs the like of which were never heard before or since. Do you ever hear her singing now? Where are her minstrels? We sometimes catch the echo of their music in Tennyson—but in him alone."

"Then you admit that *he* was a great poet?" she says.

"The greatest since Shakespeare," I answer. "And the only one who caught the matchless simplicity and strength of his songs.

> 'Come into the garden, Maud,
>     *The black bat night has flown,*'

is Shakespeare all over. And such lines as—

> 'The murmuring of innumerable bees,'

and,

> 'I move the sweet forget-me-nots,
>   *That grow for happy lovers,*'

seem fugitives from some lost play of his. Yes, Tennyson was a mighty singer. But where are his fellows? They are stumping the country, spouting on Socialism, or Woman's Rights; they are stage managing — in private theatres — 'Moralities' with an 'Im'; they are writing sciolistic essays on what we should do, and how we should do it; what we ought to eat, and what we ought to drink. They have in some occult way discovered that this world has been all wrong from the beginning, and that they were expressly born into it to set it right. They are going to set us right on everything. We have all been wrong in our ideas about the sun, moon, and stars, which, it appears, are not sun, moon, and stars at all. We have been lamentably at sea in our childish notions of Heaven and its King. The Bible, which a lot of foolish dotards died at the stake for,—which that sickly scribbler, Milton, pored over until he grew blind,—has been, figuratively, burned by the common hangman, and we are going to have a brand-new, up-to-date bible —a bible founded strictly on scientific authority."

"And what does all this point to, Mr. Dolan?" she asks.

"It indicates that England is growing old, I am sorry to say. When men change the Romantic for the Didactic, in the literature of their country, that country has seen its best days."

While we have been talking time has flown, and now, alas! the hour for departure has arrived.

"I hope we shall have a chat on literature, science, art,—not to mention Shakespeare and the musical glasses—soon again, Miss Foyle."

"Oh, yes, I hope so," she answers. "We are near neighbours. Besides, when the wedding is over, my cousin and her husband are coming to stop here, and then of course——"

Here she pulls up short, and I hasten to add—

"That will be very jolly!"

"Yes, very."

In another five minutes we three—Langton, Tempest, and myself—are driving towards the mill. Tempest is unusually silent, and Langton, giving me a nudge in the region of the ribs, whispers—

"You cut him out clean as a whistle to-night."

## CHAPTER XXI.

### CAPTAIN TEMPEST RETIRES.

ANOTHER month has gone by, and here I am still in the Mill-house. Strange to relate, Tempest also remains — confound him! I am positively certain that he stays just on purpose to annoy me.

Langton, happy fellow, is away on his wedding trip, and will not return with his bride for another three weeks. The wedding was a brilliant affair, " wid all the ouldest families in the county, begor," in full force. I acted my part of best man with great applause, and the first bridesmaid—there were eight of them—was a dream of beauty. And you should have read the special descriptive article on the whole affair, from start to finish, which, emanating from Mr. O'Hara's gifted pen, appeared in the *Ballyboyle Examiner*. To be sure it was not *quite* correct in its genealogical research *re* Langton and myself; but then, a man, even an editor, cannot know the family history of everybody.

Tempest was there, but Ethel remained close beside me. Yes, I have cut the Captain out. And now the question arises —will any other fellow cut *me* out? Ethel is miles and miles away. She, with her aunt, started for the Continent last week, having arranged to meet the bride and bridegroom in Venice, and then travel homewards with them.

"I suppose you will be still at the mill when we come back?" she said to me.

"I hope so, Miss Foyle," I answered.

And I intend to keep my word. But I cannot help feeling miserable, now that everybody is away—everybody but Tempest. What a relief it would be if he suddenly took it into his head to start for the interior of Africa!

"Are you going to remain on here?" I asked him the other morning.

"Yes, if you don't object," he answered, with one of those mocking grins. "I am going to have a few days with the trout."

And every morning finds him by the Tolka, while every evening sees him, guitar in hand, singing songs, both comic and sentimental, for Master Patrick McBride's delectation. I *hate* the man, but he has a splendid voice. If he were only member of a travelling opera company—say, somewhere in South America!

Yes, miserable—and lazy—is my condition this morning. So lazy am I that I still lie here in bed, although my watch tells me it is five minutes to nine, and the morning sun is doing its best to blind me through the window. Nice weather to visit Venice in! Fancy what the odours of the Grand Canal must be like just now!

I don't envy Langton a bit—not a little bit. What a life he *did* lead me, to be sure! Night and morning did he keep me in a state bordering on devilish madness as he expatiated on the charms of his Madge — her multifarious virtues, high culture, brilliant accomplishments, and all the rest of it! One would think that there was no other woman in the world. As if her cousin was not——

Stop, Arthur Dolan! Get up and have breakfast! The tea will be " as cowld as a corpse," to use one of Bartle's similes.

When I enter the sitting-room I find the breakfast-table only arranged for one.

"Ah," I mutter, "Tempest has been

down before me for once. I am very glad he has had breakfast. I don't feel in the best of humours this morning, and might possibly have a jolly row with him if he began any of his confounded nonsense."

I ring the bell, and presently Mrs. McBride comes in with the tray.

"Good-morning, Mrs. McBride. I am rather late for once."

"Yis, sur; an' Captain Timpist was earlier than iver he was before, havin' to ketch the thrain."

"Catch the train?"

"Yis, sur; shure didn't he tell you he was lavin' for England?"

"Indeed he did not!" I answer in some surprise. "And he started this morning?"

"Yes, sur, by the furst thrain. Lord save me, Mr. Dolan, but he was the curistist man I iver seen!"

"Yes, he was a curious mortal."

"Bedad he was, sur, all that! Whin I axed him why he was goin' to England all iv a sudden, do you know what he towld me?"

"No; what did he tell you, Mrs. McBride?"

"Why, he towld me it was his *humour!* Glory be to God! Did you iver hear tell iv such a man?"

"Never, Mrs. McBride—absolutely never! And now I shall have to breakfast, dine, and sup alone."

"Yis, indeed, sur; they have all gone an' left you all alone in your glory. Shure, the ould place won't be itself at all, at all, widout Mr. Langton an' you smokin' an' chattin' of an evenin' outside the door, an' Captain Timpist wid his guitar an' all, singin' songs to the babby. Howsomdever, Mr. Dolan, there is an ind to iverything— an ind to iverything, as me poor father ust to say—the Lord have mercy on him!"

And with this prayer Mrs. McBride leaves me to my solitary breakfast. I ought not to be surprised at anything that Tempest may elect to do, but still I should very much like to know if there is any particular meaning in his sudden departure for England. I remember now, that he received a letter by yesterday's mid-day post. Could that have anything to do with his journey?

Just as I have finished breakfast another thought strikes me, and I actually jump from my chair and pace the room twice. Then I sit down again, with a laugh at my own foolishness. Yet he *might* conceive the diabolical notion of starting for Venice! Well, even if he did, what then? He would be certain to receive the cold shoulder from Langton, and then, "where was he?" as 'Arry would say. No, I may make my mind easy on that score.

* * * * *

To my joy I received the following letter from Langton by the mid-day post. It is dated from Venice—

"My dear Dolan,

"Here we are in Venice—the Bride of the Sea, the Dream of Beauty, the City of Palaces, and, at present, the Home of Horrible Smells. We leave tomorrow for some less *eau-de-Cologney* spot. But this must be a heavenly place in the autumn. Ethel and her aunt joined us three days ago—the latter tumbled into the Grand Canal, but we fished her out all right. She told us she knew she would do that, as she had dreamt all about it.

"My wife and I have had several chats about *you*. She has made up her mind that you must get married, so prepare yourself for the slaughter! You are coming to stay with us when we return to Grange

Foyle. Ethel looks lovely — downright lovely, but she does not seem to enjoy herself very much, and I fancy will not be sorry when we turn towards home.

"Madge is calling me—good-bye.

"Yours in haste,

"JOHN LANGTON."

Good old Jack! Fancy my being under the same roof with Ethel for a regular month or so! By Jove, the thought has made me feel a new man! Ha! ha! Tempest, where are you now? You are completely out of the hunt, dear boy, with all your grinning!

Now I'll just go and have a quiet evening with the trout.

## CHAPTER XXII.

### LIZ LEAVES US.

ANOTHER week has gone by, and the travellers will return to Grange Foyle in two days, as a letter from Langton, received last night, informs me. I have been packing up my traps all the morning, and now, it being lunch-time, I go down-stairs. I see that Mrs. McBride is nursing the baby, and ask,

"Why, where is Liz?"

"Indeed, an' I don't know, sur," she answers, evidently a little out of temper. "She said she wanted to see her uncle, who she towld me was sick, an' axed me for to let her go to him, just to see how he was. Well, iv coorse I gev her lave, an' she started at tin o'clock, an' promised to be back be wan, but it's two now, an' sight nor light iv her isn't come. Wait till I ketch her—that's all!"

"Where does her uncle reside?" I ask.

"On the Ballyboyle road, sur, not more nor two mile from here. She might have been there an' back twiced sence. Wait till I ketch her—that's all!"

And Mrs. McBride leaves me, her face flushed with anger.

After lunching I quietly stroll out, and strike on to the Ballyboyle road. Then starting into a brisk walk, I soon reach a miserable cabin, with roof overgrown with weeds. Two or three half-starved hens linger about the door, scraping the dust and dirt in the vain hope of finding something to eat. Raising the latch, I push the door open and boldly enter, to find myself in a dark, filthy den, the entire furniture of which is a deal table, two "creepeens," and a heap of straw and rags. This heap is in a corner, and lying upon it asleep is a bloated, dirty-faced old man. The fireplace —a flat stone sunk in the floor—holds the ashes and fag-ends of cabbage-stalks, sticks, and other fuel of like nature.

I touch the snoring drunkard with my foot, and am answered by a grunt. Another touch, and the grunt gives place to a growl. I now turn the touch into a kick, and the sleeper is roused, and sits up staring at me in silence.

"Do you know anybody named Liz?"

"Sur!"

"Do you know anybody named Liz?"

"Is it Liz Carroll ye main?"

"Yes—nurse at the mill. Do you know her?"

"Oh yes, sur, I know Liz Carroll very well, iv coorse. She is me neice, an——"

"When did you see her last?"

" When did I see her last ? "

" Yes."

He scratches the back of his head to rouse his memory from the fumes of bad whisky, and then answers slowly—

" Oh, not so long ago, at all."

" How long ago ? "

" Oh, not so long ago, at all, sur—not so long ago, at all," he repeats, still trying to recall the exact period.

" Was it a week ago ? "

" No, thin, it was not."

" Was it this morning ? "

" Och ! not at all, sur— Whisht ! I remimber now ! It was not more nor a month ago, whin she cum——"

" Have you never seen her since ? "

" Niver, to me knowledge, sur. You know she is me neice, an——"

" That will do ! " I answer, throwing him a coin, and quitting the cabin.

When I reach the mill I go into the kitchen, where Mrs. McBride sits nursing her son in wrath.

"I have been to visit Liz's uncle," I say. "She has not been with him this morning; in fact, he has not seen her for a month."

"Lord save me, Mr. Dolan!" cries Mrs. McBride, her look of anger changing to one of apprehension. "What's got the poor crature?"

I have my own ideas on the subject, but keep them to myself.

"Do you know of any other place which she would be likely to visit?" I ask.

"Not a place, sur—not a place. Hiven sind that no harm has come to the girl! I must go an' tell himself."

"Yes; tell him to send information to the police," I say.

"Yis, sur, that I will." And away she goes.

The midday train for Dublin has nearly reached its destination by this.

The sun sinks to rest behind the wood which crowns the hill beyond the river. The rooks come cawing home to the beeches; the mill-wheel is at rest; but no Liz appears. The twilight comes, and the new moon rises. The old solemn-toned hall clock strikes nine, ten, eleven, and still no Liz comes back.

I sit by the fire smoking in the kitchen, together with Mrs. McBride, who has the baby asleep in her arms. Bartle and all the mill hands are scouring the district round in search of the lost one.

"What's got the poor crature? What's got her at all, at all?" comes from Mrs. McBride every other minute, and——

The door leading from the yard is suddenly shot open, and in rushes Shaun, white as a sheet, and with eyes ablaze.

"Where's Liz?" he demands. "Where is she? Good God, why don't you answer me, woman?"

"Shure, Shaun, agrah, I don't know," answers Mrs. McBride, turning pale, and clutching her baby close. "God knows I'd give a power to know what's got her, so I would."

"Oh, God Almighty, where is she at all!" he cries, sinking into a chair, and bursting into tears. "No man knows! No man knows!" Now he rises again, and raising his fist, exclaims, "I'll find her! I'll folly her to the inds iv the earth. Oh, Liz, Liz, me darlint—where are you?"

Down he sits again, and sobs like a child. At this moment a constabulary officer enters from the yard.

"Mrs. McBride," he says, "we have been informed that the girl you are seeking left for Dublin by the twelve o'clock train."

"Ah!" cries Shaun, starting up. "Dublin! she's gone to Dublin! I'll folly her—I'll find her! I'll folly her all over the wurrled!"

And now once again does he break down, and sinking into the chair exclaims—

"But, good God, how am I to go? How am I to go? I'd walk it, but where would she be agin I got there? Oh, Liz! Liz! me darlint! come back to a poor boy! Don't lave me all alone! Don't lave me all alone!"

As he continues sobbing, I rise, open my purse, and taking out a ten-pound note, go over and place it in his hand.

"There are ten pounds, Shaun," I say; "you can go to Dublin, and remain there too for some time."

He looks at me, and then at the note, like one half dazed; then suddenly springing to his feet he cries—

"Lord iv Hiven, it's no drame! It's a rale note—a rale note! Look at it, Mrs.

McBride! Rale money to take me to *her!*" Then turning to me he continues—" God bless you, sur! May the blessed saints in Hiven look down on you for ivermore. God bless you an' yours from this day, sleepin' an' wakin,' for ivermore."

Here he walks to the door, and turning to Mrs. McBride, says—

"Good-bye to all; I'll cum back wid Liz or niver cum back at all. God bless you all wanst more!"

And in another moment Shaun Burk is gone.

## CHAPTER XXIII.

#### ONCE MORE BESIDE HER.

I HAVE been in this beautiful old Grange Foyle for over a fortnight, though the time has flown with such swift wings that I seem to have only been here for a few hours. What talks, rides, drives *we* have had together! She has commanded that I must really and truly write a poem—she, who is a whole poem in herself, a poem bound in pink and white. But the whole surroundings breathe poetry: it comes with the scent of the pines across the park; it speaks in the coo of the wood-guest from the elms; it whispers with the rustle of the ivy against the windows.

I am down first this morning, and stand at the door watching the rabbits cutting the most extraordinary antics round one of the plantations, when I hear the rustle of a skirt behind me. How well do I know who it is!

"I see you are down first again, Mr. Dolan," she says, "but I am a good second."

"You are indeed, Miss Foyle; I am not three minutes here."

"What sleepy mortals my cousin and her lord must be!" she exclaims, putting on a little straw hat, and taking a flower-basket from the hall-table.

"Are you going to the garden? I suppose, if a man asks civilly, he may go too?"

"Yes," she answers, laughing, "you have my gracious permission."

"Thanks; may I carry the basket, please?"

She hands me the basket, and together we walk to the garden. Once there, she begins busily cutting flowers. Presently she asks, as she stoops to snip some purple pansies—

"By the way, Mr. Dolan, you never told me anything about that mysterious girl at the mill."

"Who? Alice?"

"Yes, Alice; Mrs. McBride was telling me about her."

"It was certainly a most mysterious affair," I say, "though I know more about it than Mrs. McBride."

"Indeed."

"Yes, I made it my business to find out all I could about her."

"Did you really?" she asks, still cutting those pansies. "She was rather a pretty girl, and educated, was she not?"

"Why, of course she was; that's what's

made her visit to the mill so *very* mysterious. There was not the smallest doubt about her being a gentlewoman."

Here she rises with the pansy blossoms, and placing them in the basket, takes it out of my hands, and says it is time to return to the house. Accordingly, back we go, she leading the way. When we reach the breakfast-room we find Langton and his wife awaiting us.

"Oh, there you two are!" says the latter. "What on earth has kept you all this time? We have been waiting you this hour."

"Don't mind her, Arthur," Langton says. "We have not been down five minutes."

"I'm fully aware of that," I say.

Ethel is busy arranging the flowers in a vase on the table—too busy, indeed, to speak.

"Why, Ethel, have you lost your

tongue?" asks Mrs. Langton. "You have never even wished us good-morning."

"Madge, dear, for goodness' sake forgive me!" cries Ethel, going and kissing her. "It was awfully stupid of me."

"Are you going to kiss me?" Langton wants to know.

"I don't think so," answers his wife. "Ethel dear, you keep your kisses for your own husband—whoever *he* may be."

"Yes, whoever he *may* be," Ethel echoes.

"Well, he must be somebody," remarks Miss Martha, who has just entered, "and that's something to know."

During breakfast Langton wants to know what we are all going to do with ourselves.

"I have an idea," declares his wife, "a brilliant idea—let us drive over to Killibeg and have a bathe."

"Capital idea!" cries Jack. "We'll all

join hands and sing, a life on—no, *in* the ocean wave!"

Here Miss Martha looks horrified, and the ghost of a smile flits round Ethel's lips.

"My dear John," explains Mrs. Langton, laughing, "we are not in France."

"I should think not indeed!" adds her aunt. "Mercy on me!"

"Why, I thought the Irish followed the French in everything, Miss Martha," Langton says to her, with a twinkle in the corner of his eye.

"Oh dear, no!" answers Miss Martha. "Nothing of the sort, John."

"Well, I declare, Miss Martha, you surprise me," he continues. "You completely surprise me."

"We are very old-fashioned in our customs in Ireland," I say. "Is not that so, Miss Martha?"

"Quite so, Mr. Dolan," she answers.

"Well, are there two bathing-places?" asks Langton.

"Why, of course there are," his wife tells him. "The ladies' bathing-place and the gentlemen's bathing-place are only half-a-mile apart."

"What!" exclaims Jack, "only half-a-mile? Oh, then there is no chance of us losing one another!"

So it is arranged that we start for the sea at eleven o'clock.

And that hour sees us start per wagonette, which Mrs. Langton drives (her husband sitting with her), while *we* sit alone together behind them. We take no coachman, but a groom rides behind. How time does seem to fly, to be sure! We do not appear to have been five minutes doing the five miles to Killibeg, and yet here we are, and there are the waves dancing in the August sun.

What a lovely strand it is! A long curving band of yellow sand, backed by a continuous line of alternate grey rocks and green hillocks speckled with wild pansies and lady's-purses. The tide is coming in full speed, and the waves curl and break with a joyous boom upon the slanting beach, which they rush up, and then rush down again, after offering at our feet little pink treasures never formed by mortal hands. White gulls hover above the water, flashing their wings as they wheel; and away, far, far, over the sea, the milky sails of a homeward-bound are all aglow against the blue horizon.

"How lovely!" I exclaim, as I stand gazing on the scene.

"Yes," Ethel says, "it *is* a lovely view— fit subject for a poem."

I take the hint, and mentally resolve to write some verses about sun and sea.

"Now come along, Ethel!" calls Mrs. Langton. "By the time we are ready the tide will be full."

"And for goodness' sake don't stop all day dressing!" warns her husband.

"You mind your own business!" answers his better half. "And take care you two don't drown yourselves."

"By Jove, I hope not," I say.

And so we part for a while, Ethel and her cousin proceeding to the "Ladies' First Class Bathing Establishment: Proprietor, Mrs. Casey;" while Langton and I walk along the strand towards the wooden hut which rejoices in the title of "Gentlemen's Superior Swimming Establishment." On the way Langton suddenly observes—

"Look here, Arthur—do you know what my wife says?"

"No—anything particular?"

"Why, *entre nous*, she declares that you are in love with Ethel."

"How does she know that?" I ask, turning as red as a turkey-cock.

"How do women know everything, Arthur? Come now, honour bright—is she right?"

"What do you want to know for?"

"Just to make my mind easy," he replies, taking my arm. "However, you need not answer now—I know you do."

"Do what?"

"Love Ethel Foyle."

"Oh, you know that, do you?"

"Hang it all, Arthur, what is there to be ashamed of? We are old pals."

"I am not ashamed, Jack; but what is the use of people talking about me and my love for a girl who does not love me?"

"How do you know that?" he asks.

"Oh, I'm sure of it—why should she?"

"Don't be so childishly vain and pettish, Arthur," he says. "That's the worst of you poetic fellows. You——"

"Look here, Jack, what the devil do you mean?" I ask fiercely, as I withdraw my arm from his.

This only makes the confounded beggar break into a hearty laugh. Worse still, his laughter is infectious, and I have to laugh too.

"Now listen to me, Arthur," he says, taking my arm once more. "The Ethel Stakes is an open race. You are located in the home stables, consequently you have a big pull in the weights. Take the straight office, when a cove gives it to yer."

We have now reached the bathing-place, and within another ten minutes are swimming in the cool water of Killibeg Bay.

\* \* \* \* \*

Within another hour we are all bowling

along the white road to Grange Foyle, Ethel looking like another and a lovelier Aphrodite, while her cousin's black eyes are sparkling like the waves we have left booming behind us.

"I don't know how you people feel," the latter says, "but I am starving—literally starving."

"So much the better!" declares her husband. "Shows the water agrees with you."

"We ought to have taken a lunch-basket with us," Ethel says, "and had a nice miniature picnic on the beach."

"Yes, *à la* Ramsgate," adds Langton. "But it would not be quite that without a quartette of niggers and at least one *al fresco* photographer."

"Jack, I regret to say that your tastes are extremely low," declares his wife. "Here, hold the reins, and don't let the horses run away, while I settle my back hair. It's coming down—I know it is! That dresser at the baths never *did* know how to arrange anything."

"Well, have you thought of that poem yet?" Ethel asks me.

"Yes, I am going to invoke my muse this very night."

"Really?"

"Yes, really; and you will see the result in the morning."

"Now remember, you have promised," she says.

"Yes, and I will keep to my word."

END OF VOL. I.

www.ingramcontent.com/pod-product-compliance
Lightning Source LLC
Chambersburg PA
CBHW032150230426
43672CB00011B/2504